Allan A. Glatthorn

Writing the Winning Dissertation

A Step-by-Step Guide

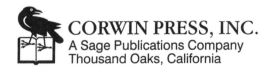

CORWIN PRESS, INC.
A Sage Publications Company
Thousand Oaks, California

The material on pp. 145-150 is reprinted from T. Husen and T. N. Postlethwaite (Eds.), *International Encyclopedia of Education* (1994), with kind permission from Elsevier Science, Ltd., The Boulevard, Langford Lane, Kidlington OX5 1GB, UK.

For information:

 Corwin Press, Inc.
A Sage Publications Company
2455 Teller Road
Thousand Oaks, California 91320
E-mail: order@corwinpress.com

SAGE Publications Ltd.
6 Bonhill Street
London EC2A 4PU
United Kingdom

SAGE Publications India Pvt. Ltd.
M-32 Market
Greater Kailash I
New Delhi 110 048 India

Printed in the United States of America

Library of Congress Cataloging-in-Publication Data

Glatthorn, Allan A., 1924-
    Writing the winning dissertation : A step-by-step guide / Allan A. Glatthorn
        p.   cm.
    Includes bibliographical references and index
    ISBN 0-8039-6677-6 (cloth : acid-free paper). — ISBN 0-8039-6678-4 (pbk. : acid-free paper)
    1. Dissertations, Academic.   2. Report writing.   3. Research.   I. Title.
LB2369.G56 1998
808'.02—dc21   97-45373

This book is printed on acid-free paper.

04 05 06 07 13 12 11 10 9

Production Editor: S. Marlene Head
Editorial Assistant: Julia Parnell
Typesetters: Laura A. and William C. E. Lawrie
Cover Designer: Marcia M. Rosenburg

Contents

Preface

A s its title suggests, this book is a practical guide to doing dissertations, one that takes you through the process one step at a
time. Having chaired close to 100 dissertations, I have learned a
great deal from all that experience, and so I set out to share those
learnings in a systematic way. I wanted to demystify the writing of
theses and dissertations, so that they would no longer be so terrify-
ing for those preparing to write these scholarly works.

The emphasis is decidedly on a *winning* dissertation. I do not
want to tell you how to write a "quickie" dissertation that you will be
ashamed of as you continue in your career. I am concerned with
helping you produce a quality study that will reflect well on you and
help you advance in your career. You will be investing considerable
time, energy, and money in this endeavor—and you want the return to reflect that significant investment.

In the discussion that follows and in the chapters themselves,
for the sake of simplicity I ordinarily use the term *dissertation* to
mean both the master's thesis and the doctoral dissertation, noting
any distinctions where they seem important. For the most part the
processes for writing both the thesis and the dissertation are similar,
differing chiefly in scope and complexity.

This book begins with the important foundation steps—from
laying the foundations for the dissertation to holding a preproposal
conference. Although some educators want to rush through these
preliminary steps, they represent a systematic way of planning carefully and laying a solid foundation. The second section of this book

focuses on the proposal, emphasizing the point that the quality of the proposal is directly related to the quality of the dissertation itself.

The third section takes you through the process of implementing the research plan and writing the dissertation. This book explains the general organizational pattern found in most scholarly reports and then examines in detail how to organize and write each chapter. The emphasis here is on doing quality research and writing a winning report. The next section concludes the process, explaining how to hold a successful defense and how to publish from the dissertation. The final section of the book identifies the problems you are likely to encounter throughout the dissertation process—problems with the committee and with your own stressors.

In general you should find it most useful if you read the chapters in order, with the exception of the two final chapters. You should read these any time you encounter problems.

Although I have attempted to write a work that will be useful for students in all graduate education programs, each institution and each chair has its own special requirements. Close and continuing contact with your dissertation chair is essential. In those cases where the chair's advice differs from mine, follow the recommendations of your chair.

Acknowledgments

In many ways this book represents a collaborative effort, even though I am the sole author. My chief debt is to all those educators with whom I have worked and from whom I have learned; I feel most indebted to all those doctoral students whom I have advised. Like most teachers I teach because it is for me the best way to learn. The professional staff at Corwin Press has been especially helpful. Gracia Alkema knows how to help authors without trying to take over. Ann McMartin provided the excellent editorial services that all authors need. And, as all writers of theses and dissertations know, there was behind the scenes a supportive and caring family, cheering me on and tolerating my absorption with the task of producing a winning book.

Allan A. Glatthorn

About the Author

Allan A. Glatthorn is Distinguished Research Professor of Education in the School of Education of East Carolina University, where he advises doctoral students, chairs dissertations, and teaches courses in supervision and curriculum. He was formerly Professor of Education at the Graduate School of Education of the University of Pennsylvania. Prior to his university assignments, he was a high school teacher and principal. In his work as a professor he has chaired close to 100 dissertations. He is the author of numerous professional books, two of which were previously published by Corwin Press.

I

Establishing the Foundations

1

Laying the Groundwork for the Thesis and Dissertation

Y ou have reached an important stage in your career, preparing to write a thesis or dissertation—a stage where many graduate students flounder. D'Andrea's (1997) study concluded that lack of structure in the dissertation process may be a key element in the failure of many students to complete their program. This book provides you with the structure you need to write a winning dissertation. Writing a winning dissertation begins with establishing a solid foundation. This chapter will help you establish such a foundation by understanding the special nature of the dissertation and making some preliminary decisions. As explained in the preface, the term *dissertation* is generally used throughout the work to refer both to master's theses and doctoral dissertations. Because there are some differences, however, it seems appropriate to conclude this introductory chapter by explaining some crucial differences between the thesis and the dissertation.

Understanding the Special Nature of the Dissertation

Like most writing, the dissertation is written to accomplish certain purposes with a specific audience, and its unique nature is perhaps best understood by analyzing purpose and audience.

Purposes in Writing the Dissertation

Purpose is perhaps best understood by examining it from three perspectives: institutional purpose, personal purpose, and communication purpose. The institutional purpose is to ensure that the degree holder has made a contribution to the field—and also to uphold an honored academic tradition. The dissertation has an ancient history, going back to the medieval university, where it was required of all those who wanted to teach. The dissertation now, of course, is perceived by the university faculty as a demonstration of the candidate's fitness to conduct and publish research—and to enter their scholarly ranks. The faculty also require the dissertation because they take seriously the mission of generating and disseminating new knowledge, and the dissertation is simply a widely accepted form for such dissemination.

You probably have several personal purposes in undertaking the dissertation. The foremost, obviously, is to earn the degree. However, you should view the dissertation as something more than an unpleasant requirement—what some students disparagingly call "the fee for the union card." You should see it also as a way of learning. In the struggle to write the dissertation, you will learn much about yourself and about the topic you have researched. Writing is a way of knowing and thinking: The process of systematizing knowledge and finding a form to express that knowledge becomes a means of discovering meaning or, as several writers have put it, "I don't know what I know until I try to write it." Such learning will foster your personal and professional growth.

Your dissertation will be a better one if you take seriously the expectation that you will make a contribution to scholarly knowledge. Even though few dissertations report earthshaking discoveries, the good ones add incrementally to the store of professional knowledge. Winning dissertations extend knowledge, even if the topic has often been studied. Suppose, for example, that a dissertation reports research indicating that cooperative learning was not as effective as whole-class learning in third-grade mathematics. That finding does not negate all the previous studies that found cooperative learning was superior. It simply says to future researchers that the issue requires additional study.

The communicative purpose is clear and simple: You write to report the results of research. You do not write to persuade, or to entertain, or to express personal feelings, but to inform. That informing function indicates that the primary quality of the writing is clarity, not creativity.

All these purposes—the institutional, the personal, and the communicative—interact to shape the dissertation in a special way.

The Audiences for the Dissertation

Your audiences are also several. You write for yourself, of course, and you must be satisfied with what you have written. When you have finished the dissertation, you should feel a sense of pride in what you have accomplished.

You write for your committee, and their predilections and idiosyncrasies must be recognized and responded to. In a way they are the most important audience, because they will scrutinize your dissertation most carefully. Although others may give it only a cursory look, the committee will examine it page by page.

You write for the faculty as a whole, and institutional standards must be met. The faculty will award you the degree, and the requirements they have set for the dissertation's form and content should be respected, even if they may seem unreasonable to you.

Finally, of course, you write for other members of your profession. Your dissertation will become a small part of a complex information network; your findings and conclusions will be read by other doctoral students and researchers in the field.

Analyzing the Special Characteristics of the Dissertation

What results, then, from this intersection of purposes and audiences is a special type of writing. The dissertation is a report of research intended primarily for a scholarly audience. It is not a longer version of a term paper. It is not an anecdotal account of your professional success. And it is not a personal statement of your philosophy or a collection of your opinions. It is an objective, documented, and detailed report of your research.

Although the specific requirements for the dissertation will vary from department to department and school to school, it is possible to identify certain general characteristics that derive from this analysis of purpose and audience.

First, dissertations are long—longer than a term paper, shorter than a book. The average length of dissertations seems to run around 200 pages, usually ranging between 125 and 225 pages.

Those are only general guidelines, of course. There are differences in fields of study: Dissertations in the natural sciences tend to be shorter than those in the social sciences. There are differences in methodology: Dissertations reporting ethnographic investigations tend to be longer than those reporting experimental studies. The practical advice here is simply to write the dissertation so that it is long enough to tell your story—without boring your committee.

Second, dissertations look scholarly—they are replete with citations of previous research. Your dissertation is expected to build upon previous knowledge, and as a fledgling research scholar you are expected to know the literature and be able to cite it appropriately. You can't simply make assertions; you have to document them. The journalist writes, "Consumers feel more confident these days." The scholar writes, "According to several recent studies, consumers surveyed report feelings of greater confidence about the economy (see, for example, Smithers, 1999; Whitney, 1998)."

Third, dissertations sound scholarly. Although there seems to be a trend away from the highly formal style and a reaction against turgid academic prose, there is still the expectation that the dissertation will sound scholarly. Your dissertation should not sound like an informal essay or an editorial; it has to sound like the writing of a scholar. And scholars write in a style that is formal, not colloquial—and objective, not subjective. The letter writer says, "We've had a lot of rain these past few weeks." The scholar writes, "Rainfall for the period June 1-30, 1999, was measured at 10.2 inches, 3.6 inches above the seasonal average."

Dissertations are also organized in a special way. Although there is increasing variation in how dissertations are organized, most still follow this time-honored pattern: Introduction, review of the literature, methodology, results, and summary and discussion. And even those that vary from this standard pattern follow a predictable order in which the variations are minor: Tell which problem you studied, explain how you studied it, report the results, and summarize and discuss the findings.

Dissertations tend to follow very specific rules about matters of style. Although instructors vary in their requirements for handling tables, writing headings, and documenting sources, there is much less variation tolerated in dissertations. Every profession has its preferred style guide, and dissertations are expected to follow those guides religiously. One of the first things to check with your dissertation chair is the style guide preferred, because most universities have their own guidelines. (Throughout this book the term *chair* is used to designate the faculty member primarily responsible for directing the research and guiding the writing of the dissertation; in many universities the term *adviser* is also used for this role.)

Making Ethical Choices With Respect to the Dissertation

There are several ethical considerations to keep in mind as you do your research and report your results.

Conduct Ethical Research

First, you must be certain that the study is consonant with generally accepted ethical principles. The following principles should be kept in mind at all times.

- *Equity.* The study does not reflect or support discrimination based on age, ethnicity, gender, sexual orientation, social class, or disability.
- *Honesty.* The study is characterized by honesty and openness. If the study requires deception, the researcher should be sure that the results will warrant the deception, that there are no alternative methods available, and that those deceived are informed as soon as possible. (See the 1990 guidelines of the American Psychological Association on this point.)
- *Humane consideration.* The study does not require or result in emotional or physical pain for participants.

Secure Informed Consent

You also should be sure to secure the informed consent of participants. *Participants* is used here broadly to mean any who are involved in your research. Suppose, for example, that you wish to conduct a study in a local elementary school of the effectiveness of a program designed to improve students' self-esteem. Here are all those who should give their informed consent: the school board, the school principal, the teachers whose classes will be involved, and any experts whom you ask to review the materials. You should also secure the approval of students and their parents, if the students' instructional program will be significantly affected. All those individuals should know what you will study, which methods you will use, and why you are conducting the study. Knowing that teachers are sometimes reluctant to complete surveys for dissertations, some graduate students will conceal that fact, pretending that the study is being done solely for professional reasons. To act in this manner is clearly unethical.

Securing informed consent is generally interpreted to mean that you will provide at the outset honest answers to the following questions.

- What will be studied?
- Why is it being studied? Indicate here that the study is being undertaken as a degree requirement.
- What methods will be used?
- Who will participate and why have they been selected?
- What are the benefits?
- What are the potential risks, if any?
- What is the time commitment required?
- Is any compensation anticipated?
- Is there an assurance of confidentiality or anonymity? Rudestam and Newton (1992) distinguish between *confidentiality* and *anonymity:* confidentiality is the assurance that no one, including the researcher, will know the identity of individual participants; anonymity is the assurance that the identity of participants will be preserved by the researcher.

A standard information form can be developed and then provided to all involved. One example is shown in Exhibit 1.1.

Acknowledge All Those Who Have Contributed or Collaborated

Another issue that needs to be dealt with at the outset is that of originality and collaboration. In your work as a graduate student, you will often work closely with and receive the help of other students and members of the faculty. Such professional collaboration has a long and honored tradition and has been the source of significant professional accomplishments. However, such relationships also

Title of Study: Assessment-Driven Instruction: Teachers' Problems and Successes

Problem to Be Studied: What difficulties do teachers experience and what successes do they achieve as they try to use instruction based on performance assessments?

Rationale for Study: Educators throughout the nation are attempting to forge a closer relationship between performance assessment and teaching. Two initial studies indicate that student achievement improves when the linkages are strengthened. However, only one study to date has documented what happens when teachers try to use assessment-driven instruction. The study will be completed as the basis for a master's thesis in education.

Methodology: Two teachers will be selected for the study. They will be asked to keep a log of their experiences. Their students will complete two surveys (attached hereto as Figures 1 and 2). The researcher will interview the teachers on three occasions—once in September, once in January, and once in May.

Participants: Two teachers who have been trained in assessment-driven instruction will be selected from volunteers. Neither their names nor the names of the district or the school will be identified in the study. One of their classes will also participate in the study.

Benefits and Risks: The benefits are both professional and personal. The study should add to the knowledge base for an important development in teaching. The teachers who participate will receive feedback about their attempts to use this new method. There are no risks involved to the teachers or their students.

Time Commitment and Compensation: The total time commitment from the teachers is expected to be 10 hours of their preparation or out-of-school time. Student surveys will require half an hour of class time. No one will be compensated.

Exhibit 1.1. Sample Information Form

raise a central issue of professional integrity. No written guidelines can ever cover all the delicate issues of who deserves credit for what. Perhaps the best guideline is one of simple honesty: Never claim credit for work that is not your own, and always give full credit to those who have helped you. The following advice is offered for dealing with some specific problems that frequently arise, both with the dissertation and with other academic papers.

1. Remember that the dissertation is expected to be an individual effort. Joint authorship is usually discouraged. If your university permits collaborative research for graduate degrees, then you should spell out explicitly the nature of the collaboration and secure the written approval of your committee.

2. Document all facts and ideas that are not commonly known and that are not original with you. This is the basic rule, of course. To it might be added the simple admonition: When in doubt, document. Keep in mind that some plagiarism is often unintentional: You have read some theoretical work; its ideas seem interesting; you remember the ideas but forget the source; when you are writing the idea reappears in the guise of an original conception. The obvious way to avoid unintentional plagiarism is to note the source when the idea first comes into your awareness. Also be sure to document all paraphrases and direct quotations, of course. These matters are more fully discussed throughout this book.

3. Accept help from anyone who wants to edit your work, but acknowledge the assistance in the front matter of the paper or dissertation. All writers (including this author) need an editor; no one is a good judge of his or her own writing. But remember that editing involves minor correcting; it is not rewriting. Don't let another student—or a professor—rewrite your materials for you, unless that person wants to appear as a coauthor. There obviously is a very fine line between editing and rewriting; your conscience is the best judge of where that line falls.

4. Secure written permission to use or quote any entire works that have been published elsewhere. Most publishers do not expect you to secure permission to quote excerpts for critical or scholarly purposes; however, you should secure permission if you reproduce

a work such as a poem, short story, entire table or figure, or if you plan to use someone else's questionnaire or survey instrument.

5. Acknowledge all assistance received. In the "acknowledgments" section of your paper or dissertation, you should acknowledge the assistance of anyone who has helped you with the content or the writing. You should acknowledge as well any outside financial assistance you have received in support of the research. It usually is wise to show the wording of the proposed acknowledgment to the person whose help is being acknowledged. Such checking prevents the embarrassment of giving too much credit to a professor (for example) who would rather not be credited or who might feel your acknowledgment should be expressed less effusively.

6. Observe scholarly norms in listing joint authorship in any articles you publish. If more than one individual has contributed substantially to the work, then that work should be published under joint authorship. In articles published under joint authorship, the authors are usually listed in the order of their contribution: The author chiefly responsible for the article is listed first; the author second in importance, second; and so on.

Report the Results Honestly and Objectively

Obviously, the most important ethical issue is not to fudge your results. Remember that in the most basic sense there are no failed studies if they are carried out carefully; even negative results are important and add to existing knowledge. Also guard against the temptation to shade the language or let your biases creep in.

Securing the Needed Resources

The other preliminary matter that you must consider is being sure that you have the resources you need.

Analyze Your Needs

First, determine if you will have the time needed to complete a winning dissertation. Ideally you should have sufficient funds so that you can work on the dissertation full-time. If that is not possible,

Item	Your Estimate
1. Tuition and fees	_____
2. Consulting services	_____
3. Hardware, software, and other equipment	_____
4. Paper and other supplies	_____
5. Books, journals, and monographs	_____
6. Telephone, fax, and postage	_____
7. Copying	_____
8. Travel	_____
Total Needed	_____

Exhibit 1.2. Budget Worksheet

then you will have to find a way to set aside extended blocks of time for your research and writing. You cannot write a winning dissertation in 1-hour stints; you need extended time periods that will enable you to warm up, get into the research and writing, and make the revisions needed.

The second key resource is hardware. You should have easy access to a powerful computer and a laser printer. Although it is possible to hire someone to do your word processing for you, that is not a good answer in considering your long-term professional career needs. Professors and educational leaders must learn to do their own word processing.

The third important resource is money. The budget worksheet shown in Exhibit 1.2 can help you make some estimates of the funds you will need. The items are explained briefly below.

Tuition and Fees. You have to pay tuition for any courses you still must take. In addition, most graduate schools require you to pay a fee during the terms when you are working on your dissertation. Although some students complain about such fees, dissertation advising is a labor-intensive process, and your fees cover only a part of the costs.

Consulting Services. You should determine if you will have to pay for any of these services: stipend for participants, word processing, data entry, data analysis, and editing.

Hardware, Software, and Other Equipment. As explained above, you will need access to a powerful computer and a laser printer. You may also need software for word processing and data analysis. Special projects may require such other equipment as a camcorder, camera, and VCR.

Paper and Other Supplies. You will find that you consume printer paper at a high rate as you write and revise.

Books, Journals, and Monographs. Even if you have access to an excellent library, you will probably want to purchase some basic references so that you can mark them up and keep them always accessible.

Telephone, Fax, and Postage. These are essential communication costs that mount as you do your research and send chapters to your committee.

Copying. You may need to make copies of instruments; you will certainly make multiple copies of each chapter.

Travel. If your research requires you to make on-site visits to distant locations, then you will need a substantial travel budget. Also keep in mind that other students may provide a helpful resource. Some students have found it helpful to develop a support group composed of students who have reached the dissertation stage. Students who responded to Meloy's (1994) survey reported that such a group was helpful to them in dealing with dissertation problems.

Search for Special Support

If you find that your needs outstrip your resources, then you should search systematically for special support. The first place to turn is to apply for a graduate assistantship. A graduate assistantship does more than provide you with extra funds; it enables you to work closely with faculty and staff, provides access to a scholarly network, and helps you develop the skills you need. If a graduate assistantship is not available, then consider applying for a grant from one of the foundations that support graduate research. The best source here is *The Foundation Directory* (Seczko, 1996), available in all research libraries.

Understand the Key Differences
Between the Thesis and the Dissertation

As noted at the outset, the master's thesis and the doctoral dissertation are both reports of scholarly investigations, completed as part of the degree requirements. All the attributes discussed above apply to both types of scholarly works. Although institutional requirements vary, there are some general differences that should be noted here. First, most master's theses are more limited in depth than doctoral dissertations. A master's thesis might report on a study of ability grouping as used in classrooms in a particular region; a doctoral dissertation might compare the effects of two grouping systems in teaching elementary mathematics. As a consequence of this difference, doctoral dissertations tend to be longer than master's theses. Also, the doctoral dissertation is likely to be more rigorous in its research methodology than a master's thesis. The thesis is more likely to seem like a "project report," explaining, for example, how a block schedule was implemented in a middle school and reporting on teachers' attitudes at the end of the year. A doctoral dissertation on the same topic might be a detailed analysis of how teachers used classroom time before a block schedule was instituted and how they used time during the first year of implementing the new schedule. Noting these differences is not to depreciate the master's thesis as a scholarly work. Many make important contributions to the field.

A Look Ahead

The rest of this book will take you through the complex process of writing the dissertation. Although the suggestions have been drawn from considerable experience in helping students produce winning dissertations, be sure that you check closely with your dissertation chair every step along the way.

2

Finding a Research Problem

Sometimes a research problem is handed to you by a research team you are invited to join: "We've been studying teacher attrition; you'll be working on attrition among teachers who have just finished their first year." Sometimes you know exactly what you want to study: "I want to know why some African American males in our school demonstrate resilience." Often, however, you will have either no idea as to what you want to study—or you will have too many ideas. This chapter will help you zero in on a good research problem.

This book distinguishes among three related terms. The term *research topic* is used here to denote a general area of study. Here are some topics to illustrate this use: learning styles, school-to-work transition, class size, charter schools, curriculum alignment. A *research problem* is a more narrowly defined issue that represents only one aspect of the research topic, such as this one: "Problems encountered in charter schools." The *problem statement* is the carefully worded research issue as it appears in the dissertation. It is even more narrow than the research problem. As explained in later chapters, problem statements may be formulated in several different ways. Here is one form that the charter school research problem might take as a problem statement: "What problems did two charter schools experience in their second year of operation?"

In general, you would move from a research topic to a research problem and then to a problem statement, as the following discussion explains. However, you may be able to take a shortcut, moving from a research problem to a problem statement. Although there will be much individual variation in the way this process is executed, you should find the following method useful for moving systematically from topic to research problem. Later chapters explain a process for defining the problem statement.

Make a Personal Assessment of Topics

You probably have some topics in mind that you have been considering. No one coming to the end of a degree program has a blank mind. You begin, therefore, by making your own preliminary assessment of the topics you have been mulling over.

Use a form similar to the one shown in Exhibit 2.1 to complete this assessment. Most students will find it helpful to rate three topics. Assessing only one or two may narrow your perspective prematurely; assessing more than three may get too complicated. Rate each topic on the basis of each criterion and then compute the total. Keep in mind that you are making only a preliminary assessment, not a final decision. The eight criteria are discussed below.

Professional Significance

What constitutes professional significance? There are no simple benchmarks. Only a scholar steeped in the literature of a given field can make a final judgment. One way to take a rough measure of significance, however, is to ask yourself, "How will it play in Dubuque?" You imagine a colleague in Dubuque, Iowa, who reads an abstract of your study. Will that colleague be interested? Or you imagine yourself being introduced to an audience of your colleagues. The introducer says, "It gives me great pleasure to introduce Doctor X, who has just completed a study of . . . " Do you feel embarrassment or pride?

There are, of course, other, more objective ways to assess professional significance. A professionally significant study makes an important contribution to the field in one of the following ways: testing a theory, contributing to the development of theory, extending existing knowledge, changing prevailing beliefs, suggesting relationships between phenomena, extending a research methodology or instrument, or providing greater depth of knowledge about previously studied phenomena.

Criteria	Topic 1	Topic 2	Topic 3
Professional significance			
Continuing professional interest			
Personal interest			
Career advancement			
Professional knowledge, experience, and skills			
Likely support			
Time required			
Accessibility			
Total score			

Code: 5, excellent; 4, very good; 3, good; 2, fair; 1, poor

Exhibit 2.1. Assessing Your Topics

Often, of course, significance inheres not in the topic area itself, but in the way it is examined. Consider these examples:

NOT PROFESSIONALLY SIGNIFICANT: "What resources are available for the study of African American literature for young adults?" The topic lacks significance because several excellent and current lists already exist.

PROFESSIONALLY SIGNIFICANT: "What images of African American males are conveyed in the juvenile literature recommended by librarians?" The topic has potential significance because research on it is likely to add to existing knowledge.

Note that the criterion speaks of significance, not originality. Some students worry unduly about trying to find a topic that has not been studied before or fret because "someone has stolen my topic." In a scientific sense, all topics are original; the replication of previous studies is a crucial part of scientific investigation. Consider this example. You are interested in principals' decision-making processes. You have tentatively identified four principals. You discover that another student wants to study the decision-making processes of those same principals. You have several ways of resolving the seeming conflict: Use different instruments and methods; find different principals; explore different aspects of decision making.

Continuing Professional Interest

The second professional criterion involves the extent to which the topic will continue to be of interest to the profession in general. The implication is that you should avoid studying educational fads—unless the study focuses on the nature of educational faddism. The hope is that you will do a study that will have value beyond the time when you receive your degree.

Consider, for example, Outcomes Based Education (OBE). Although this restructuring initiative embodied some useful ideas and was popular for a brief time, the controversy surrounding some of its value-laden ideas resulted in heated controversies that contributed to its demise. A 1994 study of its implementation would be of little interest at the current time. On the other hand, a study of school-to-work transition is likely to have continuing interest, because the problem is one that will not soon go away.

Personal Interest

Because you will be devoting a considerable amount of time to the study, obviously you should choose one that has great interest for you. Keep in mind, however, that doing the dissertation may be a way of awakening new interests.

Career Advancement

You also need to weigh the impact of your dissertation topic on your present and future career. There are three ways to view this issue.

1. If you plan to remain for an extended period of time with your present employer, then one of the main considerations is the immediate value of the topic to that employer. Therefore, you should consult with your superiors to find a topic that they believe will help the organization. For example, if your school system is experiencing continuing problems with violence in the schools, your superintendent may see a dissertation on the topic as a valuable contribution.

2. If you hope to take a leadership position in another organization and you hope to be able to consult, then the primary issue is the professional timeliness of the topic. Timeliness in this case means that it will be of great professional interest during the foreseeable future. Obviously it is difficult to predict educational trends, but you can make some reasonable assumptions about what will continue to interest educators.

3. If you hope to find a position in higher education, then the major issue to consider is its professional power. Will the topic impress search committees, enable you to publish a few articles and a book, and provide a launch pad for a research career? In essence, you ask this question: "Will this topic resonate in higher education?"

Professional Knowledge, Experience, and Skills

You can probably do the best job of researching a topic if it draws from your professional knowledge and experience and uses your research skills. For example, if you have been teaching in a block schedule for several years and believe you have found a way to make it work, that experience and knowledge would simplify your investigation.

Likely Support

The more support you have, the easier it will be to complete the dissertation. The most important source of support is your committee chair. If he or she is actively involved in researching a topic that you have chosen, then obviously you can anticipate a close working relationship. Also, as explained in Chapter 1, you might also consider whether a particular topic is likely to receive foundation or government support.

Time Required

Although time is more a factor of method than topic, you should be sure that the topic is sufficiently narrow so that it can be intensively studied within a reasonable time. At the stage of finding a topic, many students think too ambitiously, planning a study that sounds as if it might take two or three dissertations. One student, for example, talked about his topic in this way: "I'd like to research what improves student writing." The topic is simply too broad, because the factors are so complex, involving writing ability, the writing curriculum, writing instruction, and teacher and peer feedback.

Accessibility

For all studies there are issues of access. Will the school board approve of your study? Will school administrators cooperate? Does your study require parent and student approval? Will teachers be willing to answer questionnaires or be interviewed? Such issues need to be considered carefully.

Conduct a Broad Scan of the Literature

With those three topics assessed on a preliminary basis, you should next conduct a broad scan of the literature. A broad scan is the first of a three-phase review of the literature that you should undertake. Many students believe that the review of the literature occurs in one intensive period of reading. It makes more sense to see it as a continuing process. As Exhibit 2.2 indicates, each of the phases has a different purpose, and each makes a contribution to your knowledge base.

The discussion here is concerned with the broad scan. The next chapter explains the focused review; Chapter 8 examines the comprehensive critique.

Your goal for the broad scan is to increase your knowledge, so that you are better able to make a final decision about the research topic and the research problem. How much time you spend on this step will depend on the time available, your existing knowledge, the resources available to you, and how many topics you investigate. You have a choice about this last issue. If the preliminary assessment has convinced you that one topic is clearly superior, then investigate only that. If you feel torn between two of the topics, then you should

Phase	Chief Sources	Purpose
Broad scan	Reviews of the literature	To assist the researcher in identifying a research problem
Focused review	ERIC	To develop a proposal prospectus and research proposal
Comprehensive critique	All sources	To provide a scholarly foundation for the study

Exhibit 2.2. Three Phases of the Literature Review

investigate both. And if you have ample time available and feel very confused, then check out all three.

Organize for the Broad Scan

As you conduct the broad scan, organize your work, keeping in mind the following guidelines.

1. *Begin to keep a research journal.* The research journal is your personal record of your ideas, feelings, and actions as they relate to your dissertation. The journal will provide a very useful source as you do your dissertation and reflect about your progress. Here is a sample entry, to illustrate how you might use the journal:

> 4/23. Read a good article in the Summer 1997 *Review of Educational Research* on "School-to-work transitions for youth with disabilities" by L. Allen Phelps and Cheryl Hanley-Maxwell (67, 197-226). That might make a good topic; I could do a follow-up study of students with disabilities.

2. *Develop a good filing system.* You should see your filing system as a flexible one that changes as your study takes shape. You should develop a system that reflects your own way of organizing materials. You should also investigate software that makes it possible for you to computerize your knowledge base. At this stage of searching for a topic, you probably will have one general folder for each topic you are investigating. As explained in the next chapter, once you have identified a topic, then you will reorganize your files, setting up a folder for each major phase of the problem you have decided to study.

3. *Secure the approved style manual.* Check with the chair of your department to determine which style manual is to be followed. Get a copy and follow it precisely. If you have a choice, purchase and use the current edition of the *Publication Manual of the American Psychological Association* (usually referred to as the APA *Publication Manual*). Published by the American Psychological Association, it is the style manual most widely used in education.

4. *Hold on to useful sources.* Whenever possible, obtain articles, books, and monographs. Do not rely on your note-taking skills.

5. *Get full bibliographic information.* Style manuals vary considerably in relation to the information they require in end notes and reference lists; check the manual you are using to determine which information is needed. However, err on the side of completeness. For example, the current edition of the APA manual requires you to use the author's first and middle initials in the reference list, not the author's first name. However, you may decide to submit your article to a journal that requires you to include the first name; you therefore should have it in your files so that you do not have to look it up again.

6. *Begin your search record.* You should find a search record helpful to you throughout the dissertation process. A search record is what the term implies: a detailed account of the search process you used. Exhibit 2.3 shows one useful form. The search record will be help you be more systematic about your search. It can also provide the data you need for your literature review chapter. It also will enable your chair to give you constructive feedback about your search process.

Read to Inquire

At this stage, your chief purpose in retrieving and reading sources is to help you make a final decision about the topic and frame the research question. As you read, keep several questions in mind and note the answers as they become apparent to you.

- Which specific issues have been most often studied? Which seem to warrant further research?
- Which authors and which studies are most often cited?

Date of Search	Topic	Purpose	Database, Descriptors	Time Period	Results
10/4	Teacher develop-ment	Find methods	ERIC/ staff develop-ment; teachers' careers; teacher develop-ment	1980-present	Found five essential sources

Exhibit 2.3. Search Record

- What instruments are available?
- Which methods are frequently used?
- When were the major studies completed? Does the number of research studies seem to be increasing or decreasing in number?
- Which theories are used as a foundation?

This last question perhaps requires an extended comment. A theory is a set of related concepts, assumptions, and generalizations that systematically describe and explain behavior in educational organizations (Hoy & Miskel, 1987). For example, Janis and Mann (1977) developed a highly respected theory of conflict in decision making that has been used as the basis for several studies. Theories can suggest problems. For example, you might design a study that would measure how principals use what Janis and Mann describe as "defensive avoidance." The use of theory is discussed further throughout this book.

Concentrate on Research Reviews

One of the best ways to conduct the broad scan is to concentrate on research reviews. A research review is a scholarly article on a topic (such as promotion and retention) that reviews the major research studies about that topic in order to give readers a broad picture of what is known. Research reviews are usually written by eminent scholars in the field who retrieve all the sources available, evaluate the research, select the most reliable research studies, and synthesize what is known. As you search for research reviews, also look for the term *meta-analysis*. A meta-analysis is a research review that uses complex statistical processes to determine overall effects of a given intervention. There are several ways to find research reviews and meta-analyses.

- Check the library catalog to see if the library has any books whose titles begin with the words *Handbook of Research . . .* Such handbooks have been published for most of the major fields of education. For example, the *Handbook of Research on Teaching the English Language Arts* (Flood, Jensen, Lapp, & Squire, 1991) is an excellent source of reviews on that subject; its only limitation is that it does not include sources published after 1990.
- Look for a series of books entitled *Review of Research in Education*. A new volume is published each year, containing reviews of several topics. For example, Volume 22 (Apple, 1997) contains excellent reviews of research in the following areas: educational politics and policy, race and education, and teaching and research.
- Review current and back issues of the journal *Review of Educational Research*. This journal is devoted to publishing such reviews; each issue contains reviews of several topics.
- Use the library's computerized databases to search for research reviews. (A very helpful guide to computerized databases in education is Wehmeyer, 1995.) The most important database in the field of education is ERIC (Educational Resources Information Center). The database PsycLIT is useful

for any topics related to the field of psychology. In using ERIC at this stage, you may find it helpful to limit your search by using the descriptor *literature review*, along with the descriptor that identifies the topic. The "literature review" descriptor identifies any source that includes a review of the research. This is the way the search would be designated for literature reviews of the topic "teacher motivation": "SS motivation AND teachers AND DT=literature review." That command tells the computer to search for both terms (motivation, teachers) and to limit the search to the document type "literature review." (Further details about searching ERIC are contained in the manual provided at each computer station in the library or available from the reference librarian.)

- Also check the Internet. At this stage, the Internet can help you in several ways. You can use it to search ERIC and other databases. You can review course syllabi and reading lists from many university professors. You can use e-mail to contact others who are doing research in one of the topics you are considering. You also can participate in forums or discussion groups organized around one of your topics. In using the Internet, keep in mind that most of the material provided has not been screened or evaluated.

Obviously you may use other sources, if you have the time. Some students find it helpful at this stage to read dissertations on the topic. The best source for dissertations is *Dissertation Abstracts,* now available on CD-ROM. In addition to reviewing the literature and explaining the methodology, many dissertations conclude with a section entitled "Recommendations for Further Study."

Reflect and Discuss

With this preliminary knowledge base established, you are now prepared to discuss with faculty, students, and colleagues the one or two topics you are considering. Your intent here is not to let others make up your mind, but to get objective input about the topic. This is what you might say to a faculty member:

Could you spare about half an hour to help me focus on a dissertation topic? I have some tentative ideas, and I know your feedback

Research Topic	Possible Research Problem
Violence in schools	Causes of student-to-student violence
Curriculum alignment	Curriculum alignment and its effect on teacher planning
School to work	Community support for school-to-work programs
Writing feedback	Effects of peer feedback on quality of writing
Performance assessment	Problems in scoring performance assessment

Exhibit 2.4. Examples of Research Topics and Problems

would be helpful. My preliminary reading has convinced me that it would be helpful to investigate the career development of lateral entry teachers. Does that topic in general make sense to you?

You would then proceed to structure the dialogue so that you get the objective views of your partner about the most important criteria of those listed in Exhibit 2.1.

Fix on the Research Topic and Research Problem

You have made your own preliminary assessment. You have completed the broad scan, developing your knowledge base, and you have gotten input from objective sources. All those data should enable you to select a research topic. Once you have settled on a research topic, you are then ready to identify the research problem. As Exhibit 2.4 indicates, the research problem is only one of many possible approaches to a research topic; the research problem may be considered one "slice" of the topic "pie."

If you have difficulty moving from topic to problem, apply these questions to the topic you have in mind. They may suggest some profitable angles for you to explore.

- What causes it?
- Who is especially involved in it?
- When does it occur?
- What effects does it have?
- What types are there?
- How do various groups perceive it?
- In what stages does it occur?
- What will make it better?
- What makes it effective?
- What relationship does it have to other phenomena?

You can use that statement of the research problem in several of the next steps you take in the dissertation process.

3

Conducting a Focused
Review of the Literature

With the research problem identified, you should next conduct a focused review of the literature. Whereas the broad scan helped you identify a research topic and problem, the focused review will help you develop a prospectus and a proposal. A prospectus is a preliminary sketch of the proposal that will help your committee give you input for the proposal itself; the proposal is a research contract that spells out specifically for you and your committee the details of your research plan. Chapter 6 explains how to write the prospectus; Chapter 10, the proposal.

Reorganize Your Files

In identifying a research problem, you probably found it helpful to organize your files according to the topics you were investigating. In doing the focused review, you should organize your files by the divisions of the research problem you have chosen. Suppose, for example, that your research problem is "Factors influencing motivation to learn of Mexican American students." Based upon your reading, your knowledge of what the proposal will require, and your sense about the direction of your study, you might use the following categories with respect to the research problem:

- Theories or conceptual frameworks of motivation to learn
- Research methods in studying motivation to learn

- General findings with respect to motivation to learn
- Motivation to learn specific subjects
- Factors affecting motivation to learn

As you continue to review the literature, you will find it helpful to review your filing system and reorganize it as needed.

Retrieve All Related Abstracts

The next step in the process is to retrieve all the sources that are readily available. The easiest way to accomplish this step is through a computerized search of the databases available on the Internet or through your university library. For the comprehensive critique in the dissertation, you will need to throw a wide net that captures all the sources, but for the prospectus and proposal, a search of computerized databases should suffice. The one you will find most useful is ERIC because it collects sources in the field of education. If your research problem involves a psychological aspect, you might also find the PsycLIT database useful, because it focuses on psychology. Both ERIC and PsycLIT, for example, include sources on motivation.

In getting ready to use one of these databases, you should find its thesaurus helpful. In information retrieval, the thesaurus is a catalogue of the terms (called *descriptors*) used to search the database. The thesaurus also identifies other search limitations, such as type of document, educational level, and years covered. Use the appropriate descriptors to search the database, using an "abstract" format. Information specialists use three terms in specifying format. *Bibliographic information* gives you author, title, date of publication, and other identifying information about the source. *Abstract* adds a summary of the contents, written by the author of the report. *Full text* is the complete text—the entire paper or article. At this stage you should find abstracts most useful.

If you encounter any problems using the computerized database, confer with a reference librarian, who can advise you about search strategies. In addition to accessing computerized databases, you should also locate and retrieve any sources listed in the research reviews that look promising. Keep in mind that at this stage you are trying to identify the major sources, so that you are well-informed about the research on your topic. You are not trying to capture every reference.

Evaluate the Results

Now you need to evaluate the results of your search, because much of what you have retrieved will not be of use. The following guidelines should be useful here.

1. *Check the author.* If you recognize the author's name from your previous reading, the source is likely to be important. For example, any report by Robert Slavin on cooperative learning is likely to be useful, because he is considered one of the leading authorities in the field.

2. *Check the title.* If the title suggests that the article is a report of practice, the article will be less useful. Contrast these two titles: "Block Scheduling Works for Our Middle School!" "Student On-Task Behavior in Block-Scheduled Middle School Classes." The first does not sound terribly useful; the title implies that it is an enthusiastic report of one school's experience, written by one of the faculty. The second sounds like a research report. At this stage of your reading, concentrate on research studies, not reports of practice.

3. *Check the date.* In general, unless you are conducting a historical review, you should give more weight to recent studies. Here's a rough rule of thumb: For the prospectus and the proposal, emphasize the most recent 10 years.

4. *Note the source.* In general, give greater weight to journals that publish research reports and reviews. Give less weight to periodicals read chiefly by practitioners. For example, *Clearing House* is a fine periodical for practitioners, usually including articles that report on one school's experience. It tends not to publish research reports. On the other hand, the publication *Elementary School Journal* usually includes research reports. This latter journal is also a *refereed* journal, meaning that all articles must be approved by experts in the field before it is published. For the most part, articles in refereed journals will be useful.

5. *Check the document type.* In general, you should give the highest priority to those sources identified as *research report.*

6. *Read the abstract.* The abstract should give you a good idea about the potential usefulness of the source.

Based upon your analysis of these factors, code each source with one of three numbers, as follows.

1. This is a "must-have" source; it is on-target and sounds very useful.
2. This is a "maybe" source; it might be helpful and should be checked if I have the time.
3. This source is a "no" source; it is not useful at all.

Retrieve the Full Texts of Most Useful Sources

With these evaluations made, you should then retrieve the full text of all useful sources. Begin by retrieving the full text of your No. 1 sources. Here is some general advice about retrieving full text.

Books: Buy them if in print, borrow them from the library, or use interlibrary loan. The Internet lists all libraries whose catalogues are searchable on the Internet.

Dissertations: You can borrow the dissertation from the library of the university conferring the degree. You may also order it from the following: UMI Dissertation Information Service, 300 N. Zeeb Road, Ann Arbor, Michigan 48106.

Journal articles: When doing an ERIC search, you will note at the top a document number. Some are preceded by the symbol *ED*; others, by *EJ*. The *ED* denotes that the source is a research document available on microfiche. Most research libraries contain all the fiches produced by ERIC and the equipment necessary to read and print from the fiche. The code *EJ* indicates that the source is an article from a journal. You will need to consult the journal for the full text of *EJ* sources. An increasing number of research reports are available in full text by using the computer. Several of the commercial on-line services provide full text from selected journals; for example, at the time of this writing, America Online provides articles published in the journal *Educational Leadership*. Check with a reference librarian for current information.

If you find that you do not have enough No. 1 sources for your prospectus, then move to the No. 2 sources. A very rough rule of thumb is to have 15-20 sources for the prospectus and 25-50 for the proposal and the dissertation. Be sure to keep all the sources and your evaluations. You may find it necessary to retrieve those you have rated "2," and you may reconsider even the "3s." Also be sure to update your search record and continue to keep your journal.

Use Primary Sources

At this stage and all succeeding stages in the dissertation process, keep in mind a crucial distinction between primary and secondary sources. A primary source is the original report; a secondary source is an article that refers to the primary source. To illustrate the difference, consider these examples.

Cohen conducts a study on motivation and reports the results in a journal article. The Cohen report is a primary source. Jones publishes a review of the research on motivation, in which she cites the Cohen report; in this situation the Jones article is a secondary source. Good researchers do not rely on a secondary source; they search for and retrieve the primary source. Secondary sources may sometimes distort the findings of the primary source and do not provide sufficient detail.

A Concluding Note

The focused review should require 10 to 20 hours at the computer. You should find that time a good investment, because it will move you forward in the preliminary steps of writing a winning dissertation.

4

Making a Preliminary Choice of Methodology

With a clear idea about your research problem and a sound knowledge of the related literature, you next should make a preliminary choice of methodology. In doing so you should distinguish among three related concepts: *research perspectives, research types,* and *research methods.* This chapter will provide only an overview of these concepts and suggest how to make a preliminary choice of methodology. You will need to consult with a faculty member who specializes in research design and methods to be sure that your methodology is sound. Chapter 9 provides additional detail about explicating the methodology for the proposal; Chapter 16, for the dissertation.

Quantitative and Qualitative Perspectives

A research perspective, as used here, is a general view and use of research approaches and methods. There are two major perspectives: *quantitative* and *qualitative.* The quantitative perspective derives from a positivist epistemology, which holds that there is an objective reality that can be expressed numerically. As a consequence, the quantitative perspective emphasizes studies that are experimental in nature, emphasize measurement, and search for relationships. If a study uses language such as the following, it probably has used a quantitative perspective: *variable, controls, validity, reliability, hypothesis,* or *statistically significant.*

On the other hand, a qualitative perspective emphasizes a phenomenological view, in which reality inheres in the perceptions of individuals. Studies deriving from this perspective focus on meaning and understanding, taking place in naturally occurring situations (McMillan, 1996). If a study uses language such as the following, it probably has used a qualitative perspective: *naturalistic, field study, case study, context, situational, constructivism, meaning,* or *multiple realities.*

Although some researchers seem chiefly concerned with the differences between the two approaches, Morgan (1997) explains how the two perspectives can be combined. He identifies four general ways of combining the two, based upon two factors: which one is primary and which is secondary, and which one is used first and which is used second.

1. *Quantitative primary, qualitative first.* The researcher begins with a qualitative approach as the secondary method, using the qualitative data as a basis for collecting and interpreting the quantitative data (the primary method).

2. *Quantitative primary, quantitative first.* The researcher begins with a quantitative approach as the primary method, using qualitative follow-up to evaluate and interpret the quantitative results.

3. *Qualitative primary, quantitative first.* The researcher begins by collecting quantitative preliminary data as a basis for collecting and interpreting the primary qualitative data.

4. *Qualitative primary, qualitative first.* The researcher begins with the primary qualitative data, using quantitative follow-up to interpret the qualitative data.

Research Types

The term *research type* is used here to identify the general research approach. Although authorities in the field seem to differ as to how the types of research are classified, the following approaches, which are most often used in educational research, represent some of the options available to you as a researcher. To simplify the discussion, they are divided into whether they tend to use a quantitative or a qualitative perspective, although there is much overlapping in many of the types.

Studies Primarily Quantitative in Nature

The following types of research are primarily quantitative in nature.

Experimental Research

Experimental research uses methods originally applied in the physical and biological sciences. In most experiments the following procedures are used: A sample of subjects is selected, the subjects are assigned randomly to experimental and control groups, and a treatment is administered to the experimental group only. The two groups are then evaluated on the basis of the dependent variable, the consequence of the independent variable.

The latter is the presumed cause of the dependent variable.

Here is an example of an experimental design. The researcher randomly assigns 200 fourth graders to 10 classrooms. Five of those classes are randomly selected. They are given a new program on conflict resolution; the other five classes are given no program at all. At the end of the school year, both groups are administered a measure that assesses their attitudes about and knowledge of conflict resolution. Statistical techniques are used to analyze the results.

Quasi-Experimental Research

A quasi-experimental design is one that follows the general procedures of experimental research without the use of a control group or without random assignment, because random assignment or the use of control groups is often not feasible in educational settings. In a quasi-experimental study of conflict resolution, the researcher would not use random assignment but could use one of several strategies to compensate for its absence. The researcher might, for example, administer a pretest to all students, provide the treatment to half of the students, administer a posttest, and use a statistical procedure known as the *analysis of covariance* to determine if the treatment made a difference.

Causal-Comparative Research

Causal-comparative studies are designed to determine the possible causes of a phenomenon. Sometimes these studies are called *ex post facto research* because the causes are usually studied after they have had an effect upon another variable. Several studies of the effects of retention in grade use a causal-comparative design, studying the effects of not being promoted by comparing the later performance of those who were retained and those who were promoted.

Correlational Research

Correlation studies are designed to analyze the relationships between two or more variables, ordinarily through the use of correlation coefficients. You might, for example, study principals' leadership styles and teacher morale to determine if there are any statistically significant relationships between these two factors. Keep in mind the caution that correlation is not causation. Correlational studies may show a direct relationship between two factors but cannot prove causation.

Descriptive Research

As the term implies, the purpose of descriptive research is to describe a phenomenon. Although some professors depreciate descriptive studies, they can be especially valuable as one of the early stages in a research project. Descriptive studies report frequencies, averages, and percentages. For example, you might study the attitudes of teachers in public schools toward charter schools. You would not draw any conclusions about relationships; you would only report frequencies, averages, and percentages.

Evaluation Research

Evaluation research makes judgments about the merit or worth of educational programs, products, and organizations. It is typically undertaken in order to aid administrators in making professional decisions. Evaluation studies are usually described as *formative* or *summative*. Formative studies are made while a new program or product is being developed; summative studies are made when it has been completed. You might do an evaluation of a new standards-based curriculum, performing both a formative and a summative assessment.

Studies Primarily Qualitative in Nature

The following types of research tend to take a qualitative perspective.

Case Study Research

A very useful definition of the case study is that provided by Yin (1989): "A case study is an empirical inquiry that investigates a contemporary phenomenon within its real life context; when the boundaries between phenomenon and context are not clearly evident; and in which multiple sources of evidence are used" (p. 23). Although, as Yin and others point out, case studies often use quantitative measures, they more often tend to take a qualitative perspective, concerned with exploring, describing, and explaining a phenomenon. You might undertake a case study of a charter school in its first year of operation.

Ethnographic Research

Ethnographic research is a special type of case study research. It is distinguished from other types of case studies because it uses the theories and methods of anthropology to study the culture of schools and classrooms. For example, you might do an ethnographic study of the culture of a school for the deaf, attempting to understand its values, norms of behavior, rituals, and ceremonies.

Action Research

Most action research documents how an educational problem was identified, understood, and solved by practitioners. For example, you might document how you and your colleagues solved the problem of absenteeism in your school.

There are, of course, other methods employed in educational research, such as philosophical research, historical research, and legal research. Each of these has its own characteristics and uses special methods.

Research Methods

Research methods, as the term is used here, are the specific techniques used to collect data with respect to the research problem. In general, five methods are typically used in educational research.

1. *Tests and measurements.* Tests are administered and measurements are made to determine the extent of change.

2. *Interviews.* Interviews are conducted with individuals or groups to ascertain their perceptions.

3. *Observations.* Observations are made to determine what is occurring and what individuals are doing.

4. *Surveys.* Surveys are administered to assess opinions, perceptions, and attitudes.

5. *Documents.* Documents are analyzed to establish the record.

As Exhibit 4.1 indicates, the types of research explained above make more use of certain methods than of others, although there is much variation in the relationship of types and methods.

Preliminary Choices

The process explained here assumes that in developing the prospectus, you will make only a preliminary choice that may be modified through discussion with your committee. In making a preliminary choice of perspective, type, and methods, weigh several factors.

1. *The nature of the research problem.* This is probably the most important factor of all. In fact, the identification of the problem and the choice of methodology may be seen as interactive processes, with each influencing the other. For example, if you are concerned with identifying a possible causal relationship between parents reading in the home and children's interest in books, the study obviously would call for a causal-comparative study.

Type/ Method	Tests, Measurements	Interviews	Observations	Surveys	Documents
Experimental	P		A		A
Quasi-experimental	P		A		A
Causal-comparative	P		A		A
Correlational	P		A		A
Descriptive	A	A		P	A
Evaluation	P	A	A	A	A
Ethnographic		A	P		A
Action		A	P	A	
Case study		A	P	A	A

Code: **P** = primary method used; **A** = additional method that may be used.

Exhibit 4.1. Relationship of Types and Methods

2. *Your research skills.* Although it is always possible to develop new skills, you will find that designing and carrying out the study will be easier if you have mastered the required skills. If you do not understand advanced statistics, you probably should not undertake a quasi-experimental study.

3. *The research skills of your committee.* As will be explained later, it is essential that at least one member of your committee has expertise in the methodology you have chosen.

4. *Your career plans.* If you aspire to a career in higher education, you might be wiser to use one of the quantitative types, because many university faculty members are still biased in favor of quantitative studies.

5. *The time available.* In general, qualitative studies take more time than quantitative ones. Ethnographic studies are especially time-intensive.

6. *Access to the research site.* In general, school administrators will not grant access for experimental studies because parents are reluctant to have their children participate in any experiment, regardless of its promise.

5

Organizing and
Scheduling Your Work

Throughout this book you will find specific recommendations for organizing and scheduling several aspects of the dissertation project. This chapter will suggest a general planning strategy that many graduate students have found helpful. Before examining the specific suggestions about scheduling your work, you should understand the importance of realistic scheduling. As you make planning decisions, be realistic about how much time you will need. It is better to set reasonable deadlines and meet them than to set unrealistic ones that have to be changed again and again.

What is a realistic amount of time to schedule for the project, from proposal to defense? Obviously, the answer will depend upon a number of factors—such as the methodology chosen, the response time of the chair, and your own work habits. In general, most students will find that 1 year is sufficient for completing the research and the writing. Rather than depending upon such estimates, however, it makes more sense to develop a schedule that reflects your best judgments about your pace.

Develop a Planning Chart

Begin by constructing a large chart similar to the one shown in Exhibit 5.1. The size of the chart will depend upon the space available, the length of time you will need to complete the dissertation,

Strand	6/3-6/16	6/17-6/30	7/1-7/14	7/15-7/28
Adminis-tration				
Coursework				
Literature review				
Writing				
Research				

Exhibit 5.1. Sample Planning Chart

and the size of each entry. In general, a long, narrow chart about 18″ x 48″ should be best. Label five horizontal rows, as follows:

Administration. In this row, you will be noting all the important administrative requirements and actions, such as formally organizing the committee. Be sure to note the examinations you must take. Exhibit 5.2 shows the typical sequence of required actions. Be sure to check the current university catalogue.

Coursework. In this row, you will note which courses you need to complete and when you will complete them.

Literature review. You will note in this row the three phases of the literature retrieval you will complete for the prospectus (the broad scan), the proposal (the focused review), and the dissertation (the comprehensive critique). You will show in this row when you begin and complete each phase.

Writing. You will enter here when you expect to complete the writing of the prospectus, the proposal, and the dissertation. In scheduling the dissertation writing, note when you think you will be working on each chapter, ordinarily allowing 1 month for each.

Research. You will note here when you will begin and conclude the research. Chapter 9 explains the major methodological steps used in most educational research; Chapter 11 explains how to implement the research plan. Review Chapters 9 and 11 for the details

The following steps are typical ones for completing a graduate degree. Check your university catalogue for requirements and dates.

Step	When to Take It
1. Take any qualifying or preliminary examinations.	Usually after completing 9-18 semester hours of coursework
2. Complete coursework.	At your pace—limited by university regulations
3. Pass comprehensive exams.	During or after last term of coursework
4. Select dissertation committee.	When you are ready to begin serious work on dissertation
5. Hold prospectus conference.	Any time mutually convenient for student and committee
6. Apply for graduation.	Usually 4 months prior to graduation
7. Hold proposal defense.	When committee approves: draft to committee 2 weeks prior to defense
8. Hold dissertation defense.	When all members of committee approve; they should receive defense draft at least 2 weeks prior to defense
9. Submit approved dissertation to Graduate School, dean, department chair, and dissertation chair.	Usually 3-4 weeks prior to graduation

Exhibit 5.2. Completing Your Program: Steps in Sequence

you should enter in the chart. Then divide the chart into several narrow columns, each column marked with a 2-week time span. If you think you can finish within 1 year from the time you start planning, then you will need 26 columns; if you think you will need 18 months, then you will need about 38 columns. That gives you a planning chart on which you enter all the important dates as they relate to the five aspects that need to be planned.

Make the Tentative Entries

With the chart laid out, you can now make the tentative entries. Turn first to the aspect of "administration." This is where you will schedule all the administrative steps you have to take and the institutional deadlines you have to meet—such as selecting a chair, scheduling a proposal hearing, and registering for graduation. It usually seems to work best if you do this part of the planning by beginning at the end. You should therefore tentatively decide when you would like to defend your dissertation. This is the key date that will affect all others. Considering how much time you will need to do the research and write the dissertation, determine when you most likely can graduate. Then check university policies and calendars for the deadline for defenses, being sure to allow yourself some slippage. Thus, if you want to receive your doctorate in the May commencement and the university deadline for the defense of dissertations is 3 weeks prior, then tentatively aim for a dissertation defense in the first week of April. Enter that notation in the appropriate cell.

With this key date established, you can now tentatively plan for the rest of the "administration" steps. Ordinarily, you will include the items shown in Exhibit 5.2. Also note any major examinations you must pass. Check the university catalogue for the important deadlines.

Obviously, the entries you make in this "administration" row will be influenced by the policies and calendars of your own institution and your own preferences for the amount of detail you include in a planning chart. Just remember to block in all the key meetings, deadlines, and forms to be filed.

Now complete the "coursework" strand by noting all the courses you still must take and when you will complete them. Then turn to the "literature review." Indicate when you will start or have started the broad scan; then note when you have finished or will finish it. Do the same for the focused review and the comprehensive critique. The comprehensive critique is explained in detail in Chapter 8.

Now turn to the "writing" strand. In this strand you enter all the dates for writing the prospectus, the proposal, and the dissertation chapters and for submitting manuscript to your chair and the committee. Again it makes sense to do some backward planning, setting the final target first. Check your entry for the dissertation defense and decide when you should submit to your chair what you hope is the final revision of the last chapter. Ordinarily this should occur no later than 7 or 8 weeks prior to the date for the defense.

Here is the rationale for such a time lag: Your chair needs 2 weeks to read the final revision; he or she needs a few days to notify you and the other committee members that the final chapter is now approved and the defense can go forward; you or the person you have hired to do your word processing need 2 weeks to make final changes in the entire dissertation; you need 1 week to prepare copies of the dissertation for your committee; and your committee should have at least 2 weeks before the defense to read the dissertation. Obviously, this time period can be reduced by putting more pressure on yourself and your committee, but increasing the pressure at the end is a foolish thing to do. You become harried, and your committee will feel annoyed.

With that final writing target established, tentatively block in the rest of the writing deadlines, allowing yourself ample time to revise and revise again. In making these writing entries, remember that you do not have to write the chapters in the sequence in which they will appear in the dissertation. Some students prefer to get a quick start on the research and write the "results" chapter as soon as the data have been analyzed; they then write the "methodology" chapter, then the earlier chapters, and then the final chapter. Check with your chair to see if he or she has any preferences about this matter.

Now block in the important steps in the "research" strand, beginning with when you will identify the research topic and research problem. Then note when you will decide about the methodology. The other steps you enter will depend upon the methodology you have chosen; see Chapters 9 and 11 for more specifics. Again allow yourself ample time and provide for some slippage. Finally, step back and review the whole chart. Ask yourself these questions:

1. Have I entered all important university deadlines?
2. Have I allowed ample time for the chair and the committee to read chapters?

3. Have I provided for slippage and delays?

4. Have I planned realistically, allowing myself some breaks?

5. Have I taken account of any special demands of my employer that will affect my schedule?

6. Are the strands of the chart coordinated—do they dovetail with each other in synergistic fashion?

Once you have revised your planning schedule, you should review it with your chair, who can give you some helpful input based upon his or her experience in working with other students and other dissertation committees.

6

Developing the Prospectus and Organizing the Committee

The prospectus is a general sketch of your research plan, submitted to your committee before you develop the formal proposal. This chapter provides a rationale for developing a prospectus, explains how to develop it, and suggests how it can be used in organizing the committee.

A Rationale for the Prospectus

The prospectus provides a preliminary and tentative overview of your research problem and the methodology. (See Exhibit 6.1 for an example of a prospectus.)

Although many students do not bother with a prospectus, experience suggests that it is a very useful step in the process. First, it enables you to bring together and systematize all the preliminary work you have done so far. A more important reason is that it enables your committee to give you substantive input with respect to your problem and methodology before you write the formal proposal. Many students have spent months developing a proposal, only to find that the committee had different ideas about the problem or the methodology.

Mario Gutierrez   October 15, 1999

Prospectus: Doctoral Dissertation

Research topic: Performance assessments

Research problem: What problems do social studies teachers encounter in using performance assessments in the classroom?

Methodology:

RESEARCH PERSPECTIVE: Qualitative primary, qualitative first

RESEARCH TYPE: Case study

RESEARCH METHODS: The research will make primary use of observations, supplemented by interviews. Three teachers of American history will be observed during class sessions when they have decided to use performance assessments. Each teacher will be interviewed after the observation. The research will cover only the second term of the school year.

Preliminary calendar: Plans call for the dissertation to be defended in April, 2000. A detailed but tentative planning calendar is attached.

Exhibit 6.1. Example of Prospectus

Developing the Prospectus

The prospectus usually includes three elements, using the results of the processes explained in Chapters 2, 4, and 5.

- Research topic and research problem
- Methodology
- Preliminary calendar for completing the dissertation

Research Topic and Research Problem

First, identify the research topic and problem. Even if your ideas to this point have been somewhat vague, push yourself to reach resolution. Remember that the research topic is the general area you will study. The research problem is a more narrowly defined issue that represents only one aspect of the topic. Here are examples of these two matters.

> RESEARCH TOPIC: Student motivation to learn.
> RESEARCH PROBLEM: Impact of parent support on student motivation to learn.

Your committee may want you to include as well the problem statement, the carefully worded research issue as it appears in the proposal and the dissertation. (Chapter 10 explains in detail the forms that the problem statement may take.) In the prospectus, you may identify the research problem as a statement or a question, as in these examples.

> STATEMENT: The nature of decisions made by teachers in three schools using school-based management.
> QUESTION: What types of decisions do teachers make in three schools using school-based management?

Methodology

The most important component of the prospectus is the methodology. Although the preproposal conference will give your committee an opportunity to help you refine the methodology, you should be able to present in the prospectus a carefully thought-out research design. First, state the research perspective, using one of these three: quantitative; qualitative; mixed quantitative and qualitative. Next, identify the research type and the methods. Most explanations of methodology will deal with several of these issues.

- *Site of the study and means of access.* Explain where the study will be located and how you will gain access and approval.
- *Instrumentation.* Identify the instruments you will use. Include information about validity and reliability. If you plan to develop your own instruments, explain how you will test for validity and reliability.
- *Sample.* Explain who will be involved in the study and how the participants will be selected.

- *Data collection.* Explain the methods you will use to collect the data.
- *Data reduction and coding.* Explain how you will organize, reduce, and code the data. If you plan to use computer software for these purposes, identify it.
- *Data analysis.* Explain how you will analyze the data, identifying the statistical tests you will use.

If you need more specifics about methodology, review Chapter 9.

Preliminary Calendar

The final component of the prospectus is the preliminary calendar for completing the dissertation. You review the calendar you previously developed (as explained in Chapter 5) and check to be sure you can meet the deadlines identified. For the prospectus, you may include a copy of your planning calendar or a summary of your decisions.

Prepare the Prospectus for Use

Review the prospectus with these questions in mind:

1. Are the research topic and problem clearly stated?
2. Is the methodology clearly explicated?
3. Does the preliminary calendar accurately reflect my working conditions and the likely pace of the research?

Choosing and Organizing the Committee

Because the procedures of forming a committee and the policies regarding committee composition vary so much from school to school, you should know and follow those procedures and policies. However, there is a general process that has been found to be effective, regardless of specific procedural differences. (Specific suggestions for working with your committee can be found in Chapter 22.)

Timing of the Committee Selection Process

At the outset, it might be useful to discuss the timing of the committee selection process as it relates to the development of the prospectus and the proposal. In most instances you will find that this is the optimal sequence: Develop the prospectus; organize the committee, using the prospectus; develop the proposal, using committee input. Here again, the procedures of your school will influence how you handle this matter.

There are some good reasons for getting the committee organized before you develop the proposal. The proposal is a detailed research plan, and the chair should play an active role in its development. The chair's help and support at this stage can make a crucial difference. In too many cases students come to a professor with a detailed proposal that they have spent months working on and ask the professor to chair the committee. The professor says, "Yes, I'll agree to serve, but I'll want you to make several major changes in the proposal." Or, in an even worse scenario, the professor responds, "No, I don't want to direct any research that I have not designed."

Choosing the Chair

Thus, you should choose your chair early in the process—and do so before inviting other committee members. The chair plays the most important role and should have a say about the composition of the rest of the committee. D'Andrea (1997) discovered that 80.1% of the dissertation chairs surveyed indicated that they wished to be consulted on the makeup of the committee.

It might be helpful at this stage to jot down the names of three professors who are likely candidates and then rate them as your first, second, and third choices. In evaluating the faculty you are considering for chair, you can use the following criteria.

Availability. Will that professor be available during the period you will be doing your research and writing the dissertation? Here, you consider not only the professor's reputation for being available for conferences but also the professor's academic plans. Is he or she coming up for a tenure or promotion review? If so, how will the review process and the ultimate decision affect availability? Is the professor planning a sabbatical? Is the professor close to retirement?

Reputation for responding promptly and constructively. Some professors are notorious for delaying students inordinately. They sit on chapters for weeks without reading them. They demand needless and excessive revision. They change their minds often about what they expect in a chapter. Steer clear of such individuals. On the other hand, also avoid the professor who is considered too easy. Do not invite one who has low standards, who returns chapters without having read them carefully, or who wants to process students instead of educating them as researchers. With such an individual, you may finish faster, but your work won't have the quality it would have with a more demanding chair.

Interest in your research topic. Your progress will be facilitated if your chair has a genuine and strong interest in what you are researching. The chair is more likely to devote special time and effort to dissertations on a topic that he or she considers important and relevant.

Interpersonal compatibility. All other things being equal, it makes sense to work with a chair to whom you can relate. You will be working together for a year or more, and there is no point in working with someone who does not have much respect for you or is unreasonably impatient with your idiosyncrasies.

Research skills. You want to be sure that at least one person on your committee has depth in the methodology you selected. If possible, choose a chair who has that depth. If the professor you are considering for chair meets all other criteria except this one, then you probably should invite him or her to serve, knowing that you can find the methodological expertise in another committee member.

Complementarity. Does the chair complement you in important ways—can he or she give you what you need? In a sense, this may be the most important criterion. The student researcher and the dissertation chair are like a team in many respects—and what the student lacks, the chair should be able to supply. As you think of yourself as a student researcher, what do you need most from the chair? Research know-how? Access to subjects? Help with your writing? Emotional support? Professional credibility?

With your three choices ranked, you should now contact your first choice. The best way of making this contact is probably to write the professor a letter in which you indicate your interest in having him or her serve as chair, enclose the prospectus, and note that you will be calling to make an appointment to discuss the issue further. If your first choice turns you down, then go to your second and then your third choice. If you get turned down by three professors, then confer with the chairperson of the department to ask for assistance in finding someone to sponsor your research.

Organize the Rest of the Committee

Once you have resolved the issue of chair, you should give your attention to the composition of the rest of the committee. Make a preliminary list of faculty you think you might want to invite—but do not contact them until you have conferred with your chair. In making this preliminary list, consider the following factors:

- You want at least one committee member who complements the chair in terms of expertise. If your chair does not have the research depth you need, then be sure one of your committee has that depth.
- You want committee members who are generally available—who will provide the assistance you need when you need it.
- You want a committee who can get along with each other; you do not want to be caught in interfaculty crossfire.

With some names tentatively in mind, you are now ready for your first conference with the chair. This first conference with the chair should be purely an exploratory one. You do not want to resolve too many issues until the full committee has been constituted. Therefore, any initial discussion of the research problem or the methodology should be tentative and open-ended.

However, you do want to get the chairperson's input about the makeup of the committee. Some faculty are simply unable to work together on dissertation committees, and the chair should be able to indicate his or her preferences. You should therefore deal with the subject in a comment like this: "Do you have any preferences about the makeup of the rest of the committee? I've been thinking about asking Professor X and Y to serve, but I would like your input."

At this initial conference you should also explore in a tactful and sensitive manner the nature of the research relationship. There are four possibilities here. First, you will essentially carry out a piece of your chair's research. The professor will determine the specific nature of the topic and the details of the methodology. You will do the work, but the professor will call the shots and get the credit. If any publications come out of the research, your chair will appear as author and simply acknowledge your contributions.

Second, you and the chair will work cooperatively as colleagues. You will collaborate actively throughout all stages of the research and will probably coauthor any publications emanating from the research.

Third, you will play the major role throughout the research, but the chair will take an active interest in all phases.

The final possibility is that it will be your show all the way. The chair will help you finish—but do not expect much substantive help.

Obviously, you can't ask about this relationship matter directly, but you do have to probe tactfully to be sure you both understand the research relationship.

Once you and the chair have reached tentative agreement on the research relationship and the makeup of the committee, you should approach the other individuals you plan to invite. Again, write a letter and enclose the prospectus. The letter should say something like this:

> I would like to invite you to serve as a member of my dissertation committee. Both I and Professor X, who has agreed to serve as chair, believe that you could make a most important contribution. I am enclosing a prospectus that describes generally the research I propose to undertake.

That statement indicates to the faculty member being invited that the chair is on board and has discussed with you the composition of the committee. With the committee organized, you will have reached a significant milestone on your way to the dissertation.

7

Learning From the
Preproposal Conference

With the committee organized, you are now ready to hold a preproposal conference. The intent of the preproposal conference is to give your committee an opportunity to provide you with the input you need to develop a sound proposal.

Schedule the Conference

Send the committee an announcement of your intent to hold the conference, in a memo something like this:

> I would appreciate it very much if you and the other committee members would meet with me for a preproposal conference. At that time I would like to discuss my prospectus with you and solicit your input for developing the proposal. The conference will assist me in developing a sound proposal. I will be calling you during the next week to find a time and place convenient for the committee.

In discussing the conference with your chair, suggest that he or she lead the conference. You will, of course, play a very active role in the conference, but it would be inappropriate for you to lead the discussion. In carrying out your role as a doctoral researcher, manifest an attitude of professional openness. Accept the committee's suggestions as a way of strengthening your proposal.

The following discussion of the conference agenda is based on the assumption that the chair is in charge and you are playing that active and open role. As part of that active role, be sure to take careful notes throughout the conference.

Examine the Research Problem

The chair should first let you distribute copies of the prospectus as a way of structuring the conference. The chair should then give you an opportunity to explain the research problem. In doing so, you should first clarify the problem to be sure that the committee understands it fully. You then might explain your personal interest in it, indicating why it is important to you. Finally, you should discuss its professional significance. As explained in Chapter 2, a research problem has professional significance if it makes one of the following contributions to the literature: tests a theory, contributes toward the development of theory, extends existing knowledge, tests prevailing beliefs, suggests relationships between phenomena, extends a research methodology, or provides greater depth of knowledge about previously studied phenomena.

As the committee members make suggestions for refining the research problem, make careful notes and express your appreciation.

Examine the Methodology

The chair should next take you through the methodology in a step-by-step manner. Here it may be helpful to refer to the prospectus, without reading it to the group. The chair should lead the committee in examining the methodology in a very detailed manner, because the methodology is most critical in determining the quality of the dissertation. Here again, you should listen openly to their suggestions. If you feel that they are suggesting major changes that you find unacceptable, the best response is to say something like this: "I appreciate your suggestions. However, the changes you suggest are so major that I would like more time to think about them. I would like to think them over and then meet with Dr. Johnson to discuss them further."

This discussion of methodology is also an appropriate time to get the committee's input as to whether a pilot study should be undertaken before the major study. The pilot study typically involves a small number of participants and is undertaken to enable you to examine the feasibility of the study.

Review Your Schedule

The chair should next ask you to review briefly your schedule for completing the dissertation. Doing so will enable the committee to express their views about its feasibility and to ascertain whether their own plans will enable them to provide you with ongoing assistance.

Determine the Nature of the Proposal

The preproposal conference should conclude with the chair leading the committee in explaining the requirements of the proposal. The following questions should be answered.

1. *Is a comprehensive proposal or a working proposal required?* A comprehensive proposal includes the first three chapters of the dissertation. A working proposal is a shorter form, sufficiently detailed but not as comprehensive. A working proposal is recommended here, but the issue should be finally resolved in the preproposal conference, if it has not already been decided.

2. *What form should the problem statement take?* As explained in Chapter 10, the problem statement may take several forms, depending on the nature of the research problem and the methodology. The preproposal conference is a good time to resolve this issue, although the committee may give you wide latitude here.

3. *What form should the review of the literature take, and how extensive should it be?* Some committees will be satisfied with a summary of the research; others will want a more comprehensive synthesis of the literature. You should also determine if the literature review in the proposal should include a theoretical or conceptual framework. As explained in Chapter 10, a theoretical framework identifies the theory that undergirds the study; a conceptual framework explains the concepts involved in the research and shows their relationships.

4. *How detailed should the explanation of the methodology be?* As explained in Chapter 10, a very detailed explication is recommended; however, briefer explanations may be satisfactory, especially for qualitative studies.

5. *What else should be included in the proposal?* Some committees believe the proposal should also include the following components: context for or background of the problem, professional significance of the problem, assumptions, definitions, and limitations. Check with your committee about all these matters.

Follow Up on the Conference

A day or two after the conference, send the committee a letter thanking them for their suggestions and summarizing the decisions made. In fact, in all meetings with the committee make it a practice to take careful notes, systematize them for the record, and send copies to the committee.

II

Developing and Defending the Proposal

8

Conducting a Comprehensive
Critique of the Literature

B efore explaining how to conduct a comprehensive critique of
the literature, it would be useful to review the three types of literature review: the *broad scan,* the *focused review,* and the *comprehensive critique.* As explained in Chapter 2, the broad scan relies chiefly
on reviews of the literature in order to help you identify a research
problem. The focused review chiefly uses ERIC to assist you in providing a knowledge base for your prospectus and the proposal. The
comprehensive critique uses all available sources to locate any research that has a direct bearing on your research problem; it also involves the use of your critical judgment in assessing the quality of
the research. When you come to write your proposal and the literature chapter of your dissertation, you will use relevant sources located in all three phases. Those identified in the comprehensive critique will probably be most useful.

Maintain Good Research Practices
Throughout the Search

As you conduct the comprehensive critique, be sure to keep in
mind and apply sound research practices, as follows:

1. Maintain your search record. A current search record will help your chair and the reference librarians suggest additional sources.
2. Keep your research journal. Make entries that reflect your progress and your problems.
3. Make photocopies of all sources. In the comprehensive critique, you should rely on full text, not abstracts—and primary, not secondary, sources.
4. Be sure that the photocopy has full bibliographic information. Check all entries for accuracy.
5. Check the reference list of every source you have located. That reference list will give you additional leads to other sources.
6. If you store information in a computer file, back up all files.
7. Get expert help whenever you need it—from your committee, reference librarians, and other students.
8. Keep your dissertation chair informed about progress and problems.

You may also find it useful at this stage to set up and maintain a home page on the Internet so that others interested in your research problem can keep in touch with you.

Develop an Outline for the Search

Before undertaking the comprehensive critique, you should develop an outline for the search. If you have previously developed a topical filing system, as suggested earlier, you should review it to be sure it reflects your current understanding of the literature relating to your research problem. You also should review the sources you have identified, as a way of identifying the logical divisions of the problem. The search outline you develop should be sufficiently broad in scope to include all the issues that you will need to deal with in the literature chapter—but not be so broad that you sacrifice depth for coverage.

This latter point needs special emphasis. Many student researchers make the mistake of writing a review that is broad but superficial. If you read research reports in scholarly journals, you will notice that the review of the literature is narrowly focused, not broadly conceived. To clarify this matter, suppose you are doing a study on teacher leadership in curriculum. Here is an example of an outline that is much too broad:

1. The definition of *leadership*
2. The nature of curriculum leadership
3. Leadership in site-based management models
4. The nature of teacher leadership
5. The history of teacher leadership
6. Teacher leadership in curriculum
7. Teacher leadership in other areas

Such an outline includes so many topics that each issue would necessarily be treated briefly. Contrast that outline with this example, which focuses directly on the topic:

1. Teacher curriculum leadership from a historical perspective
2. Teacher curriculum leadership in elementary schools
3. Teacher curriculum leadership in secondary schools
4. Teacher curriculum leadership and its relationship to curriculum quality

This matter of breadth and depth is so critical that you should consult with your dissertation chair.

One useful way to develop the first draft of the search outline includes three simple steps. First, list all the topics that might be covered, without worrying about the order. Second, refine the list by eliminating those that seem peripheral and adding any that you might have overlooked. Finally, reorganize the refined list so that the order seems clear and logical.

Suppose, for example, that you have decided to study this research problem: Secondary mathematics teachers' use of time in the extended period schedule. Here is the comprehensive list of topics you might generate in the first step:

1. Types of schedules, traditional and innovative
2. Effect of time on learning
3. How math teachers use time in the 45-minute period

4. How math teachers use time in the extended period
5. How math teachers plan
6. The effects of the extended period on student learning
7. The types of extended periods
8. Student attitudes toward the extended schedule

Here is a refined list of topics:

1. How math teachers use time in the 45-minute schedule
2. How math teachers use time in the extended period
3. Types of extended periods
4. Factors affecting math teachers' use of time
5. Effects of extended periods on achievement in mathematics

This is how the final outline might appear:

I. Factors affecting math teachers' use of time
II. Types of extended periods
III. Effects of extended periods on achievement in math
IV. How math teachers use time in the 45-minute schedule
V. How math teachers use time in the extended period

You can use the outline as a basis for reorganizing your files and for conducting the comprehensive critique.

Establish Parameters for the Search

In consultation with your chair, define the parameters of your search. These are the issues to resolve:

1. *Type of article.* Should the search focus only on empirical research, or should it include as well other types, such as reports of practice and statements of opinion?

2. *Language and national source.* Should the search include only materials published in English? Should it include only research in the United States—or other nations as well?

3. *What time period should the search cover?* In general, searches for theses and dissertations will usually cover the period from 1980 to the present. Historical studies, of course, cover a longer period of time. The topic itself might impose some time limitations. For example, you would probably not find articles on the extended period schedule before the mid-1980s.

4. *Should the review include theories and conceptual frameworks?* As explained more fully in Chapter 10, the review of the literature ordinarily should include a review of theories and concepts, but your committee may feel that they need not be included in your proposal.

Conduct a Comprehensive Search

In conducting the comprehensive critique, remember that your goal is to locate all existing sources that relate to your research problem. Completeness is not important in the broad scan or the focused review—but it is for the comprehensive critique. The following discussion assumes that you have filed in an organized manner the results of your search of research reviews and of the ERIC database.

1. *Use the Internet and commercial on-line services.* The Internet can assist you in several ways. Many dissertations are now abstracted in the home page of the university where the degree was awarded. The Internet also gives you access to educational databases. Also, you can communicate with other researchers through "forums" or discussion groups. Commercial on-line services provide many of these sources, but impose access and use charges, whereas the Internet is free except for connect charges.

2. *Use other computerized sources.* Check with the reference librarian in your university library to determine what other computerized data sources are available. Most research libraries will include the following sources on CDs:

- *Dissertations Abstracts.* Most dissertations will be abstracted here. You will also find information about ordering dissertations.
- *PsycLIT.* As explained previously, PsycLIT is a database that includes research on topics in the field of psychology. Because

many educational topics involve psychological issues, be sure to check this database. It has its own thesaurus, the *Thesaurus of Psychological Index Terms*. Using this thesaurus to identify search descriptors will greatly simplify the search process.

- *Books in Print Plus*. This database includes bibliographic information about all books still in print. You can look up your research topic in this reference.
- *Essay and General Literature Index*. This source will help you locate chapters in books, although it does not comprehensively cover the field of education.
- *UnCover*. This source provides the table of contents pages of nearly 17,000 journals, including most of those in the field of education; it is maintained by the Colorado Alliance of Research Libraries (CARL). It is a useful source for locating current publications that as yet may not have been entered in the ERIC database.

3. *Search for current conference papers.* Papers presented at the annual conferences of such organizations as the American Educational Research Association are often not entered into the ERIC database until a year or two after they were first presented. You should attend such conferences, being sure to get a conference program. If you cannot attend, order a copy of the program from the association. When you identify a paper that looks useful, write to the author a letter something like this:

> Please send me one copy of the paper on "Resilience in African American Males" that you presented at the 1999 conference of AERA. I could not attend your session, unfortunately. I am currently writing a dissertation on the topic and am sure that your paper would be most helpful in my own research. I would be most happy to pay any charges involved.

Be sure to send a thank-you note if the author sends you a copy of the paper.

4. *Read current journals.* Each month you should make a regular check of journals in your field, especially those that often include research reports. Also read the newspaper *Education Week*; it usually includes very timely news about research reports just published.

Critique All Sources Retrieved

You have retrieved all the sources that seem to relate to your research problem. Now you should critique those sources to be sure that your review of the literature includes only sound research. The reader expects a critical review, not an indiscriminate collection. Although you can make some tentative judgments about research quality from an abstract, you can develop a valid critique only on the basis of a careful reading of the full text.

In undertaking that careful reading and keeping a record of the results, you should find the form shown at the end of this chapter in Exhibit 8.1 useful. It was developed by reviewing several texts in research methods. (McMillan, 1996, was especially helpful.) Notice that it first lists criteria that apply to most research and then notes those criteria specific to a given type. Complete the form and then attach it to your copy of the source.

This careful critique of the research will enable you to make some important decisions as you prepare to write the literature review. What is the overall quality of the research on this topic? Which studies should receive major attention? Which studies are so flawed that they should be ignored? Which issues require further study?

A Concluding Note

Conducting a comprehensive critique will be an ongoing process throughout the dissertation project. Although time-consuming, it is an essential step that should not be hurried. Your goal is to know everything published so far on your research problem—and to know which sources satisfy appropriate criteria. The knowledge you gain will help you write a sound proposal, write a quality literature chapter, and develop your own professional knowledge.

Authors:_____ Publication date:_____

Brief title:_____

Overall evaluation:

_____ Sound in all respects
_____ Generally sound, with some minor flaws
_____ Seriously flawed

Research Problem: Research problem clearly stated; problem researchable.

Evaluation: _____

Comments:

Literature Review: Theory or conceptual framework presented; literature review comprehensive; literature review free of bias; studies summarized accurately and in sufficient detail; previous research synthesized, related to research reported.

Evaluation: _____

Comments:

Subjects: Clearly described; method of sampling described; selection free of bias; selection procedures appropriate; adequate number (usually at least a 60% response rate required for survey studies).

Evaluation:_____

Comments:

Instrumentation: Valid, with evidence for validity presented clearly; reliable, with evidence presented clearly; instruments described fully; administration procedures indicated; norms

Exhibit 8.1. Form for Evaluating Sources

or standards specified; scores meaningful, without distortion; observers and interviewers trained and qualified.

Evaluation: _____

Comments:

Data Collection, Presentation, and Analysis: Data collection method described clearly, free of bias; data reduced appropriately; data presented clearly; data analysis clearly explained, supported by data presented.

Evaluation: _____

Comments:

Summary and Discussion: Summary accurate, sufficiently detailed, without distortion; findings interpreted appropriately; conclusions warranted by findings; interpretations clearly identified as such.

Evaluation: _____

Comments:

Criteria Specific to Research Type:

EXPERIMENTAL AND QUASI-EXPERIMENTAL: Hypothesis clearly stated; direct manipulation of independent variable; design clearly explicated; extraneous variables controlled.

CAUSAL-COMPARATIVE: Causal condition previously occurred; extraneous variables controlled; differences between groups controlled; causal conclusions warranted.

CORRELATIONAL: Causation not inferred; size of correlation sufficient for use of results (group predictions require .40-.60; individual, .75).

DESCRIPTIVE: Conclusions about relationships not made; graphic representations accurate without distortion.

Exhibit 8.1. Continued

EVALUATION: Evaluation model identified; client and stakeholders specified; criteria specified; sources for criteria explained; standards clearly explicated, justified; evaluations rendered, supported with specific data.

CASE STUDY: Researcher's role identified; possible bias acknowledged, controlled; descriptions differentiated from interpretations; multiple methods of data collection and sources used; study of sufficient duration.

ACTION RESEARCH: Researcher's role identified; bias acknowledged; actions clearly described; actions evaluated, with adequate evaluation data provided; multiple perspectives and data sources used.

Evaluation on type-specific criteria: _____

Comments:

Exhibit 8.1. Continued

9

Detailing the Methodology

Chapter 4 explained how you should make a preliminary choice of methodology and provided an overview of research perspectives, types, and methods. In this chapter you will learn how to develop your methodology in detail. The chapter first explains the general nature of the research design and then looks more closely at the research types and their related methods used most often in educational studies. (The discussion that follows draws from several sources: Goetz & LeCompte, 1984; Hubbard & Power, 1993; Merriam, 1988; McMillan, 1996; Smith & Glass, 1987; Yin, 1989.)

The Research Design: Its General Nature

Regardless of the type of research you use, you should be certain to develop a sound research design. A research design is a specific plan for studying the research problem. The following elements are commonly found in all research designs:

1. *The research perspective.* Indicate if the research is quantitative, qualitative, or mixed.

2. *The type and subtype of the research.* Identify the general type, as well as specify the subtype. For example, it is not enough to indicate that you will do a case study; you should also specify the subtype, such as ethnography.

3. *The context for the study.* Indicate where and when the study will be conducted and whether access has been assured.

4. *The participants in the study.* Identify who will be involved in the study, as in this example: "The study will focus on five teachers in the English department; they have all agreed to take part in the study."

5. *The methods and instruments used to collect data.* Explain how you will collect data—by document or archive examination, interviews, testing, observations, or surveys. Indicate the specific instruments, if any, that will be used. This example shows how the issue might be treated: "Data will be collected by observations and interviews. The researcher will make weekly observations of all teachers and interview them in focus groups."

6. *Data analysis.* Explain how you will organize, reduce, analyze, and display the data you have collected. Both quantitative and qualitative studies require an explication of how you will handle the data analysis. (For comprehensive treatments of data analysis, see Smith & Glass, 1987, for quantitative studies, and Miles & Huberman, 1984, for qualitative research.)

The Research Design: Type-Specific Issues

Although the above features are common to all designs, they take quite different forms depending upon the research type. To aid you in explicating your methodology, each of the major types of educational research is noted below, with the specific questions you should answer.

Experimental and Quasi-Experimental Research

As explained in Chapter 4, experimental research uses methods originally developed and applied in the natural sciences. Most experimental studies are intended to establish cause-and-effect relationships. Here is an example: Does accommodating the learning style preferences of middle school students improve their reading ability? In quasi-experimental research, the researcher uses in general the same methods but cannot use random assignment of subjects to treatment groups. A quasi-experimental study might answer a question such as this one: Does teacher praise improve the self-esteem of African American youth? If you propose to undertake an experimental or quasi-experimental study, you should answer the following specific questions in addition to the general issues noted above:

1. *What subtype will be used?* Most experts in research methods identify four subtypes, each of which differs in design details: single group, true experimental, nonequivalent groups, and factorial.

2. *How will the subjects be selected?* If random methods will be used, how will randomness be ensured?

3. *How will the subjects be assigned to experimental and control groups?* If random assignment is planned, how will randomness be ensured? If randomness is not planned, how will you deal with the problem that the groups will not be equivalent?

4. *Will pretesting be used?* If so, what test will be used?

5. *What treatment will be applied to the experimental group?* How long will the treatment last? What specifically will be done, by whom? How will you ensure that the treatment will be applied as intended?

6. *How will the dependent variable be measured?* Remember that the dependent variable is the likely result of the independent variable introduced earlier in the study.

7. *What inferential statistics will you use to establish relationships?*

8. *What methods will you use to control for threats to internal validity?* Internal validity refers to the extent to which the researcher could claim that the independent variable caused the dependent variable. Research experts have identified several threats to internal validity, such as the following: history, maturation, testing, and instrumentation.

9. *What methods will you use to control threats to external validity?* External validity is the extent to which the findings can be legitimately

generalized. Experts have identified several threats to external validity, such as the Hawthorne effect, experimenter effect, novelty effect, and task effect.

Causal-Comparative Research

Like experimental and quasi-experimental research, causal-comparative research (sometimes called *ex post facto research*) attempts to establish cause-and-effect relationships. However, the researcher has much less control over the independent variable and cannot use randomness in selection and assignment. For example, a researcher might use causal-comparative research to attempt to establish a causal relationship between teenage smoking and participation in athletics.

The methodology should answer the following specific questions:

1. *What subtype will be used?* Four subtypes are frequently used: between-group, time series, path model, and archival time series.

2. *If between-group design is used, how will the homogeneity of groups be established?* If a path model, what theory will be used as the basis? For archival time series, how will you control for history, maturation, and mortality?

3. *In the interpretation of results, how will you avoid the post hoc fallacy*—assuming that because one factor preceded another, it must have caused the other?

Correlational Research

Correlational studies attempt to understand patterns of relationships among variables. Although such studies cannot prove causation, they are useful in predicting one variable from another or building a theory about a complex phenomenon. Correlational research would be used to answer this question: "How are television viewing and out-of-school reading related?"

In detailing the methodology, respond to the following issues:

1. What subtype will be used: bivariate correlations, multiple regression, discriminant analysis, partial correlations, and factor analysis?

2. How will the variables be measured? How will the validity and reliability of the measures be established? Why were these variables selected?

3. How will data be displayed? Will scatter plots or correlation matrices be used?

4. What correlation statistics will be used? Why were they chosen?

Descriptive Research

Descriptive research is used to describe the characteristics of a population by directly examining samples of that population. Descriptive studies make primary use of surveys, interviews, and observations. They are usually undertaken in the early stages of a phenomenon. Thus a researcher might decide to use descriptive research to answer this question: "What are the distinguishing characteristics of teachers who choose to teach in a charter school?"

These are the special questions to address, in addition to the general design issues noted above.

1. How will the sample be selected—convenience, volunteer, quotas, or probability sampling?

2. What variables will be studied? Why were they selected?

3. If a survey will be used, what response rate will be required? How will you deal with the problem of nonresponse bias?

4. What statistics will be used to report results? How will data be displayed?

Evaluation Research

Evaluation research makes judgments about the merit or worth of educational programs, products, and organizations and is usually undertaken to assist administrators in making professional decisions. Although evaluation is considered here as a type of research, many research experts distinguish between research and evaluation. For example, Smith and Glass (1987) note these features that they believe distinguish it from research: It is parochial, in the sense that it focuses on a single entity; it examines multiple aspects of the unit being studied; it often originates with a client, not the researcher; it is often undertaken when a decision must be made.

Of all these distinguishing features, the parochialism of evaluation seems to be the major obstacle in justifying it as research. Thus, a study is not likely to make a significant contribution to knowledge if it reaches a conclusion of this sort: "Product X is inferior." However, an evaluation study can escape the limits of parochialism if it accomplishes one or more of the following purposes:

- Provides an early test of a new approach or model of evaluation
- Develops an instrument that can be used in other studies
- Evaluates a program that is widely used but has had little systematic evaluation
- Documents how the evaluation results were used by groups of stakeholders

An evaluation methodology should address the following specific issues:

1. Who are the clients—who initiated the request for evaluation?
2. What evaluation model or theory will be used?
3. Who are the stakeholders—who has an interest in the results?
4. What criteria will be used? How were they derived?
5. What standards will be used to make judgments?

Case Study and Ethnographic Research

Case study research is undertaken to provide a detailed description of a particular situation, organization, individual, or event. It is disciplined inquiry concerned with illuminating meaning by using inductive processes. As one type of case study, an ethnography uses the methods and theories of anthropology to understand the culture of an organization. For example, you might undertake an ethnographic study of an alternative school, delineating its values, norms, symbols, and celebrations.

Deal with the following issues in explaining case study methodology:

1. What subtype will be used—ethnographic, historical, psychological, or sociological?
2. Will the study verify existing theory or generate new theory?
3. What community or intact group will be studied? Will the study focus on an individual, small work groups, single classroom, school district?
4. What will be the role of the researcher? Many case study researchers identify themselves as "participant-observers."
5. What type of interviews, if any, will be used—key informant, focus group, life history?
6. How will the researcher provide for triangulation? *Triangulation* is used to mean a process of using multiple perspectives and data sources.

Action Research

Action research is usually carried out by a researcher who is deeply involved in the processes of identifying and solving an educational problem. Some action researchers study their own teaching or leadership processes. Others focus on colleagues or students. Many work on problems in their organization.

Action research methodologies should deal with the following specific issues:

1. What is the goal of the action research?
2. What will be the focus of the action research?
3. What is the role of the researcher?
4. What procedures will probably be used to solve the problem?
5. What procedures will be used to document and evaluate the actions taken?
6. How will you guard against researcher bias?

Developing Your Research Design

One useful way of developing your research design is to begin by identifying the research perspective, as explained in Chapter 4. Then analyze your skills, the resources available, and the nature of the problem to decide tentatively about the research type. Use the input from the preproposal conference as well as the general and specific questions in the above discussion to sketch in your research design. At that point in the process, you should consult with a faculty member who is known to be an expert in the research type you have selected. Ask the faculty member to critique your design; make the necessary revisions and additions. You will then be ready to explicate the details of the design in the proposal, as explained in the next chapter.

10

Developing and Defending the Proposal

If you have followed all the steps explained in the previous chapters, you should find it a relatively simple matter to develop and defend your proposal. Also, if you have worked closely with your committee throughout these processes, there should be no anxiety at all about what might go wrong. This chapter, then, helps you tie together all those steps into a strong research proposal that you can defend without problems.

As you work on your proposal, keep in mind its importance. It is an implicit contract between you and the committee. You are expected to carry out the research as proposed, unless the committee approves changes you request. And the committee is expected to evaluate the dissertation on the extent to which you carried out your proposal. If, for example, your proposal did not specify the use of focus groups, a committee member should not criticize you at dissertation defense time for not using focus groups.

Developing the Proposal: The Big Picture

Although universities vary in their proposal requirements, almost all proposals include three major components: introduction to the study, review of the literature, and methodology. Observe that the overall organization of the proposal follows the conventional sequence of the first three dissertation chapters.

Two types of proposals are used in graduate research. The *comprehensive proposal* is a very detailed and full description of the proposed research. It essentially represents the first three chapters of your dissertation. The *working proposal* is a briefer form that has only enough detail to get you started in the research. To clarify the differences between the two, Exhibit 10.1 shows how the length of each section might vary in typical comprehensive and working proposals. Note a few major features of the figure. First, the working proposal is about one third the length of the comprehensive proposal. Second, the two proposals include about the same amount of detail in the methodology section; the major differences between the two types of proposals are in Chapters 1 and 2.

Obviously, it is essential for you in the early stages of developing your proposal to ascertain the committee's preferences about this issue. Some committees prefer the comprehensive proposal because all the details are worked out before the research begins. Often, a year or more is spent developing the comprehensive proposal; however, much less time is then devoted to completing the rest of the dissertation. Other committees prefer to have the student use the working proposal, because they want the student to reduce the time developing the proposal and increase the time doing the research. The working proposal is more often used in qualitative research, because many qualitative studies use an emerging design in which the methodology changes as the research moves along.

In writing either the comprehensive or the working proposal, remember to use the future tense, not the past tense, in referring to your study. The dissertation, on the other hand, uses the past tense. Here are two examples:

PROPOSAL: "Focus group interviews of 10 teachers will be conducted."
DISSERTATION: "Focus group interviews of 10 teachers were conducted."

Developing the Proposal: Writing Chapter 1

The first chapter of the proposal introduces the research proposal. In the full proposal, the first chapter usually includes these elements: introduction to the chapter, the background of the study,

Chapter	Comprehensive Page Length	Working Page Length
1. Introduction to the study	20	5
2. Review of the literature	40	5
3. Methodology	15	15
Appendix: Proposed timeline	1	1
Total	76	26

Exhibit 10.1. Length of Comprehensive and Working Proposals

the problem statement, and the professional significance of the study. The full proposal also may include the definitions of key terms and the delimitations of the study. The delimitations are the limitations you have imposed on the study that limit generalization. The working proposal usually includes in its first chapter the introduction, the problem statement, and the significance of the problem.

Introduction to the Chapter

The chapter begins with one or two paragraphs that serve only to get the reader into the chapter. The simplest way to accomplish this goal is to state the purpose of the proposed study. Here is an example: "This working proposal describes a proposed research study that will examine the nature of decision making in schools that have used site-based management for 3 years or more. This first chapter of the proposal introduces the study."

Background of the Study

The background presents to the reader the context for your study. Usually it explains what external factors might influence the study. In this sense the "background" section says to the reader, "Here is what was happening in education that affects the study." For example, a 1998 study of how a district used curriculum standards to develop its curricula would probably be influenced by these background factors: the continuing concern for curriculum quality, the increased activity of the states in developing standards, and the expanded role of professional organizations in developing standards. Some committees also expect the discussion of the background to explain how your proposed study will contribute to the knowledge base.

In identifying the background factors, ask yourself the following questions:

- What trends are occurring in this field?
- What new developments are most promising?
- What problems are surfacing in most schools?
- What societal developments are affecting the schools?
- If someone reads this proposal 25 years from now, what would the reader want to know about the background?
- What is the general state of knowledge about the research problem?

In most proposals, a discussion of three background factors would be sufficient. In the comprehensive proposal, each background factor you have identified would be explained fully in a page or more. The working proposal does not have to include an examination of the background, unless the committee requires it.

The Problem Statement

As explained in Chapter 2 of this book, the problem statement is a very clear formulation of the research problem. Because the way the problem is formulated will affect the organization of both the proposal and the dissertation, you should give special attention to its formulation. You have several choices about the form of the problem statement.

Hypotheses. Many problem statements include *hypotheses*. A hypothesis is the researcher's prediction or expectation of what the results will show. In research, hypotheses involve two or more variables, such as time on task and achievement. Hypotheses are derived from theory. As you review the literature about your research problem, you should look for theory-derived hypotheses. When the hypothesis is stated in positive form, it is often termed a *research hypothesis*. Here are some examples of research hypotheses:

- There is a positive relationship between students' use of computers in learning mathematics and their achievement in mathematics.
- Students retained in first grade will have lower achievement in mathematics than those who are promoted.
- There is a positive relationship between first-grade students' achievement in reading and the time parents spend reading to them at home.

In experimental and quasi-experimental studies, the problem is often framed as a *null hypothesis*. A null hypothesis is a negative form of the hypothesis; it is a statement that the differences have occurred because of chance. The research study will determine if the null hypothesis is rejected or accepted. Here is an example of a null hypothesis: "There is no correlation between the extent of teachers' autonomy in developing curricula and students' achievement in science."

Research question and hypotheses. Many correlational and causal-comparative studies frame the problem statement as a research question followed by the research hypotheses. Here is an example:

RESEARCH QUESTION: Does teacher involvement in decision making affect teachers' morale?
RESEARCH HYPOTHESES:
1. Teacher involvement in decision making varies from school to school within a district.
2. Teacher involvement in decision making varies with decision-making content.
3. Teacher involvement in decision making affects morale in a positive direction only in certain schools and only with certain types of decision-making content.

General purpose of the study. Many case studies frame the problem statement as a general purpose. Because the case study typically uses an evolving design, the case study researcher is often reluctant to be overly specific at the proposal stage. Here is an example: "The purpose of this ethnographic study is to observe, describe, and analyze the culture of a charter school as it develops in its first year of operation." The general purpose mode can also be used in action research, as in this example: "The purpose of this action research study is to plan, develop, and evaluate a conflict-resolution curriculum for students in a community college."

Single question. Many qualitative studies frame the problem statement as an open-ended question. Here is an example: "In what ways do students use the Internet when they are working independently on the computer?"

General question followed by two or more specific questions. In order to achieve greater specificity, the researcher may use an open-ended question supported by its related more specific question. Here is an example from an evaluation study: "The general question this study will attempt to answer is this one: Is the curriculum audit an effective and feasible tool for educational change?" That general question subsumes several related questions, as follows:

1. Is the audit feasible in terms of fiscal costs?
2. Is the audit feasible in terms of participant time?
3. Is the audit effective in the change process from the perspective of administrators?
4. Is the audit effective in the change process from the perspective of teachers?

In general, you should take the following steps in developing a clear and functional problem statement. First, identify a research topic. Read enough so that you are able to refine the topic as a research problem. Then make a decision about the methodology. With the general method selected, then decide what type of problem statement would be most appropriate. Throughout the process check, with your committee. Exhibit 10.2 indicates the typical relationships between type of research and type of problem statement.

Professional Significance of the Study

Both the working proposal and the comprehensive proposal should include a section explaining the professional significance of the study. This section in a sense answers these related questions: "Why is the proposed study worth doing? What professional value

Research Type/ Problem Statement	Research Question and Hypothesis	Null Hypothesis	General Purpose	General Question	General Question and Specific Questions
Experimental and quasi-experimental	Sometimes used	Usually used			
Causal-comparative	Sometimes used	Usually used			
Correlational	Sometimes used	Usually used			
Descriptive			Sometimes used	Sometimes used	Usually used
Evaluation			Sometimes used	Sometimes used	Usually used
Case study, ethnography			Usually used	Sometimes used	Sometimes used
Action			Usually used	Sometimes used	Sometimes used

Exhibit 10.2. Research Types and Problem Statements

will it have?" In this explanation, be sure that you do not speak to personal or local reasons, such as the following:

- The district has adopted a new program.
- I was involved in the piloting of an extended period schedule.
- The school was moving to interdisciplinary curriculum.

Instead, you should speak to the contribution your study will make to professional knowledge. As explained in Chapter 2, a professionally significant study can contribute in one or more of these ways: test a theory, contribute to the development of theory, extend existing knowledge, change prevailing beliefs, suggest relationships between phenomena, extend a research methodology or instrument, or provide greater depth of knowledge about a previously studied phenomenon. Here is an example of how this issue of professional significance might be handled:

> It is hoped that this proposed case study of differentiated supervision will make a contribution to the knowledge of alternative models of supervision. Although there have been many anecdotal reports from school districts using the differentiated model, such reports have relied primarily on surveys of administrators and teachers. Although several doctoral studies were conducted in the late 1970s, there have been no case studies reported in the literature since 1990. (For the earlier studies, see . . .)

The researcher would then continue to develop this line of reasoning, pointing out why additional case studies are needed.

Other optional components. As noted above, some committees will require you to include in Chapter 1 of the proposal the delimitations and definitions. Check with your committee whether these are to be included.

Developing the Proposal: Writing Chapter 2

In the typical proposal, Chapter 2 is the review of the literature. In the comprehensive proposal, the review of the literature is an in-depth synthesis of the knowledge base of your research problem. If you develop a comprehensive proposal, then in writing Chapter 2 of the dissertation you need only to update the proposal review. If you use the working proposal, the synthesis can be much briefer, as explained below. Both the working proposal and the comprehensive proposal should review the theoretical and empirical literature.

Reviewing the Theoretical Literature

Your proposal should include a review of the theoretical literature. The theoretical review should provide a basis for the empirical review that usually follows. You can accomplish this goal by reviewing the theories typically used in studying the problem you have identified or by developing a conceptual framework.

Reviewing theories. A theory is a series of concepts organized into assumptions and generalizations that lead to hypotheses about a phenomenon. Hoy and Miskel (1987) note several uses of theory: It guides research in a problem area, it facilitates understanding and analysis of complex phenomena, it aids practitioners in making decisions, and it provides a basis for predicting what might occur. For example, Janis and Mann's (1977) theory of conflict and decision making is useful in understanding under what conditions stress has a negative effect on the quality of decision making and when individuals use sound decision-making procedures to avoid making choices. The Janis-Mann theory has been tested in several studies of administrative decision making.

In the proposal, you should review briefly the major theories related to your problem and then explicate in depth the one theory that you believe will be most useful in your own study. For example, a proposal to study decision making by a site-based management team might use the following outline:

I. Review of theories of decision making
   1. Classical theories of decision making
   2. Administrative theories of decision making
   3. Incremental theories of decision making
II. Analysis of Janis-Mann conflict theory
   1. Concepts
   2. Assumptions
   3. Generalizations

The review of theories in the comprehensive proposal might require about ten pages. In the working proposal, a one-page list of the major theories and a one-page review of the theory you have selected should suffice.

Developing a conceptual framework. A conceptual framework is typically derived from theory. It identifies the concepts included in a complex phenomenon and shows their relationships. The relationships are often presented visually in a flow chart, web diagram, or other type of schematic. For example, Exhibit 10.3 shows a conceptual framework developed by this author that explains what the teacher does in a particular class. The conceptual framework was developed

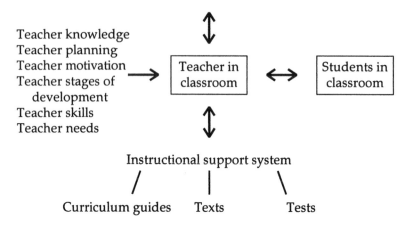

Exhibit 10.3. Factors Influencing Teaching

by reviewing the extensive literature on the factors influencing teaching.

A careful reading of the literature should help you develop a conceptual framework. You should first identify the major concepts involved in the phenomenon. Then you should identify the more specific subconcepts related to the major ones. Next you should discern how the concepts and subconcepts are related. With that knowledge base established, you should experiment with several different visual representations of the concepts and their relationships. You should then choose a visual representation that will best show how the concepts and subconcepts are related. Finally, you should write a clear explanation of the visual representation. In the comprehensive proposal, the presentation and discussion of the conceptual framework might require five pages; in the working proposal, a one-page visual accompanied by one page of explanation should be sufficient.

In developing your proposal, you should confer with your chair to determine if you should include either a review of theory or a conceptual framework—or both.

Reviewing the Empirical Literature

The review of the empirical literature is an important part of the proposal. It is included in the proposal not simply to meet a traditional requirement but, more essentially, to link your proposed research with the prior research. As noted in Exhibit 10.1, the literature review of the working proposal is relatively brief, compared with that of the comprehensive proposal. Regardless of length, both proposals should include the components discussed in this section.

Link the review of the literature with the theoretical or conceptual framework. Remember that the review of the theory has been done as a way of structuring the review of the empirical literature. You should therefore make the connection explicit. Suppose, for example, that a student researcher who proposes to study how student behavior affects teacher performance has developed the conceptual framework shown in Exhibit 10.3. The student might make the connection in the following manner.

> As noted in the conceptual framework, a teacher's performance in any given class is a result of several interacting factors. Of all those factors influencing the teacher, the behavior of the students has perhaps received the least attention by researchers. Because student behavior is the focus of the proposed research, the review of the empirical literature that follows will review all the published studies on the interaction of student behavior and teacher performance.

Organize the review of the empirical research. Your review will be more effective if it has a clear organization. Simply listing the studies is not sufficient. You have to organize the studies in some coherent manner and make that pattern clear to your reader. In general, you can organize the review in one of the following ways:

1. *Chronological.* Use a time pattern if there have been trends or developments in the knowledge base over time. For example, a review of the literature on Outcomes Based Education might use a chronological order, because there were definite trends in its use over a 20-year period.

2. *Opposing camps.* If you are reviewing an issue about which researchers have reached different conclusions, then it might be helpful

Mentor Problems		
Researchers	*Date*	*Finding*
Feiman-Nemser & Floden	1986	Expert status of mentors questioned in the culture of teaching
Smylie & Denny	1989	Expert status not accepted by rest of teachers

Exhibit 10.4. Summary Form Emphasizing Researcher

to organize them accordingly. If, for example, you propose to study the grouping of academically gifted students, you might organize the review in this manner:

   a. Studies supporting homogeneous grouping
   b. Studies supporting heterogeneous grouping

3. *Conceptual.* Perhaps the most common pattern of research reviews involves a conceptual analysis, in which you identify the major concepts or factors appearing in the literature. For example, the research on teachers' professional development might be organized in this manner:

   a. Studies of teachers' cognitive development
   b. Studies of teachers' moral development
   c. Studies of teachers' career development

Be sure to make clear to the reader which organizational pattern you are using.

Review the research. You next use that organizational pattern to review the research. The review in the comprehensive proposal should be fully developed, with studies described sufficiently for the reader to understand their findings. In the working proposal, you could use either of two summary forms. Exhibit 10.4 shows a

---

Mentor Problems

1. Mentors are given an expert status. However, in the culture of teaching, such status is suspect, because teachers tend to have an egalitarian perspective (Feiman-Nemser & Floden, 1986; Smylie & Denny, 1989).

Exhibit 10.5. Research Summary Emphasizing Findings

form that emphasizes the researcher; Exhibit 10.5, one that emphasizes the findings.

Relate the review to your study. Finally, be sure to relate the review of the research to your own study. Make clear to the reader the connection between what has been learned in the past and what you propose to do. Here is how one student researcher made that connection: "As the above review indicates, teachers tend to have negative feelings about curriculum monitoring systems. This proposed study will examine whether those negative feelings are found when teachers are held accountable for student achievement on end-of-course tests."

Developing the Proposal: Writing Chapter 3

Chapter 3 includes a detailed explanation of the proposed methodology. Note that both the full proposal and the working proposal present the methodology in detail. Along with the problem statement, the explanation of the methodology is the most important part of the proposal. Presenting the methodology in full detail accomplishes two goals: It enables you to systematize your decisions about the methods you plan to use, and it enables your committee to ensure that the methodology is sound.

Be sure to organize the discussion of the methodology in a logical manner. Although the specific organization will vary with the type of research, in general the following pattern will apply for most studies:

1. Type of research and specific subtype
2. Context and access
3. Participants and how selected
4. Instrumentation
5. Data collection
6. Data analysis

Review Chapter 9 for a discussion of the specific issues to be examined in the methodology section.

Developing the Proposal: The Appendix Section

The appendix section will include any supporting materials, such as copies of instruments. It should also include a copy of your planning schedule or a summary of it.

Holding the Proposal Defense

The proposal defense should be a relatively simple matter if you have followed the procedures explained in previous chapters. The assumptions are that you have held and profited from a preproposal conference and that you have done the additional work required.

Preparing for the Proposal Defense

The defense will go well if you make certain preparations. First, prepare a good draft of your proposal. Ask the chair to review it before you submit it to the other members. Make any revisions suggested by the chair. Then confer with the chair to review the structure of the proposal defense and to identify other issues. The Proposal Conference Agenda Form shown in Exhibit 10.6 should help you prepare for and participate in the proposal conference. The issues noted in the form are discussed in the following sections.

Structure of the Proposal Defense

The structure of the defense will depend on the norms of your institution and the preferences of your committee. The form will help you and the chair clarify the major structural elements. Ordi-

Student's name:_____ Date of conference:_____

Time and location of conference:_____

Research problem:_____

Dissertation committee:_____

Preproposal conference: Has a preproposal conference been held? If so, summarize its outcomes.

Conference Structure

1. Who will lead the session?_____

2. Who will be responsible for making notes of decisions made?_____

3. How long will the session probably last?_____

4. About how much time should the student take to present the proposal?_____

Other Conference Issues

1. Does the suggested timeline for completion seem reasonable?

2. What procedures should be followed in circulating chapters for committee review?

3. What style manual should be followed in writing the dissertation? In the dissertation, how should the student-researcher refer to himself or herself?

4. How should the dissertation be organized?

5. What should be the scope of the literature review?

Exhibit 10.6. Proposal Conference Agenda Form

narily, the dissertation chair will lead the proposal defense and will also note for the record any decisions or recommendations made.

However, the chair may wish you to take a leadership role and to take your own notes. Most proposal conferences will last 1 hour; some may require additional time if major problems occur or if differences arise among the committee members.

You should take about 15-30 minutes to present your proposal. A working proposal will probably take less time than a comprehensive proposal. Taking less than 15 minutes will seem too cursory; taking more than 30 minutes is simply unnecessary, assuming that your committee has read the proposal.

Dealing With Other Defense Issues

After the proposal itself has been reviewed, you should ask the chair to discuss with the committee the issues noted in Exhibit 10.6, if the issues have not previously been resolved. The committee should let you know if the timeline for completion seems reasonable from their perspective. Will they be available for reviewing chapters and meeting with you? The issue of how chapters should be circulated is a critical one. The following procedure is efficient both in saving everyone's time and in maximizing committee feedback.

1. You send Chapter 1 to your chair.
2. He or she reviews it and suggests revisions.
3. You revise and submit the revision to the chair, who reviews it and approves it (unless additional changes are needed).
4. You then use the same procedures with Chapters 2 and 3, in succession.
5. When the chair has approved the first three chapters, he or she notifies the other committee members that those chapters are ready for their review.
6. You send the other committee members the approved drafts of Chapters 1, 2, and 3.
7. The other committee members send their suggestions for revision to the chair, who reviews them and confers with you about additional changes required for Chapters 1-3.
8. You revise Chapters 1-3.
9. You write Chapter 4 and send it to the chair, who suggests revisions.

10. You revise Chapter 4 and send the revised chapter to your chair.
11. You write Chapter 5 and send it to the chair, who suggests revisions.
12. You revise Chapter 5.
13. Your chair notifies the committee that all chapters have been approved and that you are ready for the dissertation draft.
14. You send the completed dissertation to the committee.
15. You make any final changes the other committee members request.

This set of procedures should simplify the complex process of working with your committee. However, be sure to resolve the procedure issue with the committee; do not assume that they will agree to use the procedures described above.

The proposal defense is also a good time to resolve the issue of writing style. Most education professors prefer that student researchers use the current edition of the APA *Publication Manual*. One specific issue of writing style is how you should refer to yourself. The traditional style is to minimize the person of the researcher by using the passive voice of the verb or by using the term *the researcher,* as in these examples: "The tests were administered." "The researcher then interviewed the principal."

However, many scholars now believe that a more direct style is preferable: "I then administered the tests." "I interviewed the principal."

You should also clarify the issue of dissertation organization. Here is the standard organizational pattern used in most quantitative studies:

1. Introduction to the study
2. Review of the literature
3. Methodology
4. Results of the study
5. Summary and discussion

However, this standard pattern does not work for many qualitative studies. For example, a case study of a math department might be organized in this manner:

1. Introduction to the study
2. Selecting the site and gaining access
3. Phase 1: Making contact
4. Phase 2: Getting to serious work
5. Phase 3: Winding things up
6. Summary and discussion

The other key issue you should resolve at the defense, if you have not done so previously, is the scope of the literature review. Does the committee prefer a broad review of all related issues or an in-depth, narrowly focused review? Also determine if the literature review should include an explanation of the search process you used and a review of the theoretical literature.

III

Researching and Writing the Thesis or Dissertation

11

Carrying Out the Research Design

With the proposal defense concluded and the necessary revisions made in the proposal, you are now ready to carry out the research design. This chapter will suggest some steps you can take and some problems you can avoid in this critical part of your study.

Communicate Periodically With the Chair

A common complaint of dissertation chairs is the student's failure to communicate. In too many instances, the student completes the proposal defense, encounters family and career problems that cause delays, and does not communicate with the chair for several months. The recommendation here is to send to the chair a brief report every 2 weeks, even if there is nothing of significance to report. Most committee members will not require frequent communication; they assume that the chair is monitoring the student's progress. To simplify communication, you may wish to use your own version of the form shown in Exhibit 11.1.

It is especially important to communicate with both the chair and other committee members if you plan to make major changes in the problem statement or the methodology. You should detail the proposed changes in a memo to the committee, requesting their written approval. Remember that the approved proposal is a contract between you and the committee.

| Student: Mario Gonzalez | | | |
| Chair: Dr. McCarthy | | | |
Research Step	Date Proposed	Date Accomplished	Comments
Orient teachers	9/20	9/23	Principal requested postponement; 3 teachers expressed concern about privacy

Exhibit 11.1. Research Progress Report

Ensure Access to the Research Site

Before beginning data collection, check again on your ability to gain access to the research site. In some cases, district administrators or school boards change their minds about permitting the study. Usually they worry that parent opposition is building—or the study seems too intrusive. To minimize such occurrences, ask them to sign a written statement granting approval before you begin data collection. They are less likely to change their minds once they have agreed in writing to grant access. If they do deny access after initial approval, appeal the decision while making plans to find another site.

Avoid Premature Data Collection

Some students make the serious mistake of beginning the data collection before the proposal defense has been held. Although their desire to get a quick start on the research is understandable, this premature beginning is fraught with risks. The committee will be unhappy that their function has been short-circuited. Lacking final committee review, the instruments may be flawed. Proper access may not have been obtained. In the unlikely event that the committee approves data collection before the proposal defense has been held, secure a written statement to this effect from the chair. If you have collected a substantial body of information without committee approval, apologize for your impulsiveness, review with them what you have collected, and ask them to help you bring into line the data collected and the problem posed.

Develop a Detailed Planning Calendar

As suggested in Chapter 5, you should have developed a general planning calendar. Now it is time to develop a more detailed calendar for implementing the research. Exhibit 11.2 shows a calendar one student developed for a correlational study that examined the relationships between body type and peer social acceptance. In developing the calendar, indicate realistic deadlines that you are sure you can meet. Ask your chair to review your detailed calendar. Then do your best to adhere to the deadlines you have set.

Change the Schedule as Needed

You should be ready to change the schedule as the need arises, especially from alterations at the research site. Most doctoral studies in education involve schools and their faculties. As an educator, you know how unpredictable life is in such situations. The most common result is a change in the school's schedule. Perhaps you had planned on a faculty meeting to be held in September as a time to orient the teachers, but the principal cancels the meeting—or decides there is no time for your orientation. Plan a research schedule that is flexible and allows for slippage. Reschedule your work as needed. In doing so, be sure that you do not alienate the administrators or teachers; your study is not the most important aspect of their professional lives.

Step	Date
1. Confirm access.	6/1
2. Secure copies of instruments.	6/15
3. Prepare orientation materials.	7/1
4. Orient teachers.	9/20
5. Orient students.	9/27
6. Administer student instruments.	10/1, 10/2
7. Administer teacher instruments.	10/1, 10/2
8. Compute and standardize student scores.	10/15-10/30
9. Compute and standardize scores.	11/1-11/15
10. Use statistical packages to compute correlations.	11/16-11/20
11. Review all data for accuracy.	12/1-12/15

Exhibit 11.2. Research Planning Calendar

Prevent Problems With the Intervention

Many researchers have discovered to their dismay that the teachers did not implement the intervention as planned. Teachers tend to be independent when it comes to their classes, and many believe that they can do a better job than the researcher in implementing an intervention. You can take several steps to avoid problems of this sort.

Throughout the research you should emphasize to the teachers that you see them as highly skilled professionals who are making a professional contribution by collaborating with you as equals. Whenever possible, you should involve the teachers in the planning process so that they feel some ownership of what is done. Also, you should provide them with the training needed to implement the intervention as required. Some researchers have even developed written scripts for the teachers to follow, when fidelity of implementation is crucial to the research.

Use Computers Mindfully

Most graduate researchers use the available software to aid in the data analysis process. Several packages are available for both quantitative and qualitative analyses; check with your committee about the best package currently available. However, you should use the software mindfully—that is, you should understand the processes at work. Understanding the processes will facilitate your interpretation of the results and will also enable you to respond thoughtfully at the defense, if an issue of data analysis arises. Here are two examples to illustrate what is meant:

Mindless Use of Software Package. I used SPSS to do a *t* test. It wasn't significant. Committee member asks, "What is the *t* test?" The *t* test is a test of significance.

Mindful Use of Software Package. I used SPSS to compute the *t* test. Committee member asks, "What is the *t* test?" The *t* test is used to see if the observed difference between the mean scores of two groups on a measure is likely to have occurred by chance—or if it represents a true difference in the scores of the populations.

Ensure a High Rate of Return on Surveys

Many student researchers develop survey studies and then, to their dismay, secure only a low rate of return. Cochran (1977) showed that even nonresponse rates of as low as 20% may be sufficient to raise questions about the generalizability of the results. Although most experts in the field believe that researchers should aim for a 60% return, Smith and Glass (1987) point out that some surveys with response rates lower than 50% are valid because there are no differences between responders and nonresponders, whereas some surveys with a 90% rate are biased.

You can prevent the problem of nonresponse by using an instrument that is very clearly written and easy to complete. You are also more likely to get a satisfactory return rate if you can convince the participants that your study is important and assure them that you will share the results with them. You can also ensure a high rate of return by having participants complete the survey instrument while they are part of an intact group, such as a faculty meeting.

If the initial rate of return is low, you will have to follow up with tactful reminders. If nonrespondent rates are lower than 90% even after two reminders, Smith and Glass recommend that you perform a *nonrespondent bias check* to determine if the nonrespondents differ significantly from the respondents on key variables.

Maintain Careful and Duplicate Records

Throughout the study you should keep the researcher's journal and the search record. In addition, you should be sure to make backup files and copies of all data. Although losing data is not a common occurrence, the problem occurs frequently enough to stress the importance of copies and backup files.

12

Mastering the Academic Style

Before examining the issue of how to write specific chapters of the dissertation, it might be useful at this juncture to take a close look at the general goal of mastering the academic style. The academic style is a style of writing that is expected in term papers, theses, dissertations, and scholarly articles. Notice that this book is not written in an academic style, because it is intended as a technical manual of advice written for graduate students.

Following the Recommended Style Guide

At the outset, be sure you have available and refer to the approved style guide. Check with your chair to see which one is recommended. If you have a choice, use the most recent edition of the APA *Publication Manual.* Also observe the following guidelines specified by UMI Dissertation Services. (See Chapter 19 for additional details.)

1. Use high-quality white paper, minimum 20-pound weight, 8 1/2" by 11". Do not use erasable stock.
2. Double-space all text. Long quotations and footnotes may be single-spaced.
3. Use a 10-point or 12-point font.
4. Use a letter-quality printer.
5. Do not use correction fluid or tape.

Most style manuals also recommend that you use a left margin of 1 1/2 inches to provide room for binding.

Using the Writing Process

Mastering a basic process for writing should help you at all stages of the dissertation. And what you learn here about using a good writing process for the dissertation should be of use to you in future academic writing tasks.

Which writing process should you use in writing the dissertation? The answer is a complex one, because individuals vary so much. There is not too much guidance from the research. There are several studies of how professional writers write novels and hundreds of studies of how students write essays—but few studies on how graduate students write theses and dissertation. In addition, the standard process model taught to secondary students (prewrite, draft, edit, revise, publish) is not useful when it comes to writing dissertations. However, by reviewing the available research and by reflecting on personal experience, it is possible to offer some general guidelines that should stand you in good stead.

Develop an Effective Approach to Writing

Before looking at the specific tasks of writing one chapter, it might be useful to consider some general guidelines for developing an effective approach to writing. First, ensure that you have ready access to a computer and good word processing software. The computer is no longer a fascinating toy or a technological luxury; it is a scholarly necessity. It can greatly facilitate the writing process: It can make revision a relatively simple matter, give you access to databases, and take over the data analysis task. As a consequence, it can reduce significantly the time you spend in doing the dissertation. Then, when you have finished writing the dissertation, it can continue to be of immeasurable help in your professional career. The point here is to liberate yourself from dependence upon secretaries or dictating machines.

Next, create a research-writing center for yourself. Your research and your writing will go better if you can carve out at the university or at home a special spot of your own where you do all your dissertation thinking and writing. Equip it with your research and writing needs: computer, files, dictionary, and related professional works. Finally, reserve the center only for dissertation work, so that every time you sit down in that special chair, the environment says "dissertation time."

Also, develop a writing schedule that will help you write systematically and effectively. Because the general issue of developing and following a schedule was discussed in an earlier chapter of this book, it is probably sufficient to note here the need to schedule longer blocks of uninterrupted time on a regular basis—and to keep that time inviolate. Most writers find that they need at least a 3-hour block of time to get some good writing done. You begin with a slow warm-up period, in which you struggle to get going. Then you hit your stride and find the flow. If you have to stop just when you feel your writing is going well, you will lose the momentum. Therefore, your writing time should be free of distraction: You can't write while you're watching the baby, doing the laundry, or watching television.

Finally, arrange for the help you will need. If you do not do your own word processing, you may need to hire a professional word processor. If you do hire someone, make clear that you are contracting for word processing services, not "typing." You want your dissertation on diskettes, to simplify all the revising that will have to be done.

You will also need an editor. An editor's function is to read very carefully your good drafts and suggest or make specific improvements in organization and style. The editor does not write for you; that is dishonest and unethical. But the editor does more than put in commas and correct your spelling. A good editor will suggest how the chapter might be reorganized, will note paragraphs that need fuller development, and will indicate how sentences can be rewritten. Every writer needs a good editor—and making use of a good editor will simplify the whole process for you. You should, of course, acknowledge the editor's help in the appropriate place in your dissertation.

This matter of using editing assistance is so delicate, however, that you should check it out with your chair. Some universities provide specific policy guidelines to help students distinguish between the ethical practice of using an editor and the unethical one of using a ghost-writer. And some chairs may prefer that you not use an editor. In general, however, professors do not want to edit your writing themselves. They are scholars, not editors.

Write With an Efficient Process

With that basic approach well established, you are ready to write one chapter. What is the best process to use here? As noted above, there is no single right answer. You have to experiment to find the process that works best for you. In general, however, you should find the following process a useful one.

Begin by systematizing your knowledge. The first step is to review and systematize what you know about the contents of that chapter. Think about what you have learned. Review your notes on the reading you have done. Take a fresh look at your results. In this stage of systematizing your knowledge, you may find it helpful to talk into a tape recorder, think aloud, or discuss with a colleague. Or you may simply read and reflect. The important thing is to call to mind what you know and start to think about a systematic way of ordering that knowledge.

Next, plan your chapter. With your knowledge reviewed and tentatively organized, you now should plan the chapter. How do you plan? You can simply adopt one of the outlines suggested in later sections of this work, because dissertation chapters tend to follow certain basic organizing patterns. You can read other dissertations like your own and follow a pattern that someone else has used. (Do not worry about the ethics of following someone else's plan; professional writers do it all the time.) Or you can start from scratch and develop your own plan. If you start from scratch, there are two basic ways of developing a plan. Some writers plan from the bottom up: They review their notes, put the notes in similar piles, identify the general topic of each pile, and then find a logical order for the general topics. Other writers plan from the top down: They think about the contents of that chapter in an analytical fashion, determine the broad topics that need to be treated, and decide on a logical arrangement.

Regardless of the method you use, it probably is a good idea to reduce your plan to a written topical outline. You should ask your chair to review the outline before you start to write that chapter; if the chair prefers not to review outlines, then ask a colleague whom you respect. The important rule to remember is that you should not start writing a chapter until someone else has reviewed your outline. You may be convinced that your outline is excellent—but you are too close to your material to be a reliable judge of that matter. You need the input of someone who is objective. Unless your chair requires a particular outline form, you should use any outlining system that is clear to you and find others who will read it.

Then begin to write. Check your outline. Review your notes for the first section. Then start to write that section, without worrying too much about style. What do you do if you have "writer's block"—that frustrating feeling that all writers know at times, when the words just will not come? The best answer is to write your way through it. Grit your teeth and write whatever comes into your head. Force yourself to write, even if the writing seems bad. Do not sit there and worry that you cannot write. If you do not know how to start the chapter, skip the introduction and jump right into the first major idea. As you write, use headings and verbal signals to make your organization clear to the reader. The appropriate use of headings will help the reader track your organizational pattern. To understand this point, consider Exhibits 12.1 and 12.2. Exhibit 12.1 shows part of an outline of Chapter 2 of a study on student questions; Exhibit 12.2 illustrates how the headings are used to clarify the organization. You should also use verbal signals that show where the chapter is going, such as *first, next, also, finally*.

You should also revise as you write. Most good writers revise as they write, following a procedure that goes something like this:

Write a paragraph.

Stop and read what was just written.

Revise that paragraph.

Write another paragraph—and start the cycle all over again.

How much revising you do and what you revise for as you write are individual matters. Some writers are perfectionists. Especially if they are working on a word processor, they will correct punctuation, tinker with sentences, fuss with word choice. Others do a quick draft without any revising—and then polish the entire draft.

With that first draft finished, the best advice is to put it aside for a few hours at least—and then read it with a fresh eye. Pretend you are the reader, not the writer. See if the organization is clear, if the generalizations are well supported, if the sentences flow clearly and smoothly, if the words sound right. Then revise to improve.

In the revising process, use the editing processes available with your word processing software. All will do a spell-check. Just remember that spell-check programs will not detect an error such as

I. Types of student questions

    A. On task

        1. Clarification

        2. Solution checking

        3. Extension

    B. Requests

    C. Diversions

II. Frequency

    A. By subject

    B. By grade level

        1. Elementary

        2. Middle

        3. High

Exhibit 12.1. Partial Outline of Review of Literature: Student Questions

using *affect* when you should have used *effect*. Most programs will also provide a thesaurus, if you wish to avoid repeating a word and cannot think of an alternative. You can also use a style checker such as *Grammatik* that will suggest revisions, based on the kind of style you have indicated.

After you have revised, give the chapter to your editor. Before sending it on to your chair, be sure your editor has had a chance to review it. Discuss any substantive changes with your editor and then revise in accordance with the editor's suggestions and your own sense of what you want to do.

Now you can send the revised chapter to your chair, along with an outline. At this point, you will need to follow your chair's recommendations about the submission of chapters. Some chairs prefer to get one chapter in good shape before letting the other committee members see it; others prefer to get committee input at the draft stage. Even if your chair does not require an outline, it probably is a

2. Review of the Literature

This chapter will review the literature on student questions, as a means of providing an intellectual background for the present study. The chapter organizes the review by examining the studies relating to four aspects of student questions: types of student questions; frequency of questions; teacher strategies to elicit questions; and effects of student questions.

Types of Student Questions

Researchers have categorized student questions in terms of three purposes: to accomplish the task; to make a request; and to divert the teacher from the task.

Accomplishing the Task

Students ask questions to enable them to accomplish the assigned task. Task-oriented questions tend to be of three types.

Questions of clarification. Most of the task-related questions involve questions of clarification. Reeves (1987) found that elementary students asked such questions more often than secondary students . . .

Exhibit 12.2. Headings Corresponding to Outline

good idea to include one anyway. The outline shows that you have planned systematically and helps your chair read and respond.

Most students find it helpful to include with their revised chapter a copy of the chair's or committee's previous suggestions for revision. That strategy should minimize the problem of receiving conflicting messages with each subsequent revision.

Mastering the Academic Style

Academic writing is a unique genre that has its own norms. And one of the implicit expectations of doctoral programs is that you will learn to write like a scholar. This section of the chapter will offer some general advice about the sense of self you wish to project and then will deal with more specific applications.

Project an Appropriate Persona

Any discussion of the scholarly style should probably begin with an analysis of the scholarly persona. The persona is the public person you present in the writing—the image created by the writing. It results from several factors—the things you choose to write about, the tone you adopt, the sentences you write, the words you use. As a writer of a dissertation, you want to project the persona of a scholar; your writing should convey a message something like the following: "The writer is an informed and knowledgeable person who knows the norms and conventions of the profession, who has done some interesting and useful research, but who has the good sense to be suitably modest about it."

Below are listed some general suggestions for achieving such an effect:

1. *Strive for clarity.* Many writers of dissertations get caught up in the struggle to sound scholarly and, in the process of trying to achieve that effect, become confusing. The best scholarly writing is lucid, even to someone not expert in the field. Clarity is essentially a matter of ordering your sentences so that the parts clearly relate to each other and choosing your words so that they are readily understood. Clarity also comes about when you arrange the parts in a systematic way and make that arrangement clear to the reader.

2. *Project maturity.* Your sentences should sound mature. The discussion below will explain how such an effect is achieved; the point here is that your concern for clarity must be balanced with a concern for maturity. You could write in a very simple style that would be clear and easy to read—but it might sound just a bit too immature for the readers of your dissertation.

3. *Project a sense of formality.* As pointed out in an earlier chapter, the dissertation is expected to be more formal in its style than most of the writing that you do. Although there is a clear tendency away from the stilted formality that characterized most academic writing just a decade or so ago, there is still the expectation that you will not sound informal or colloquial.

4. *Strike an appropriate balance between confidence and tentativeness.* Many dissertation writers fall into the trap of claiming too much. The problem they have studied is the most important one, the need is most urgent, the study proves beyond a doubt that such a finding is true. The answer here is to use the language of tentativeness: *it is likely that, it seems obvious here, one tentative conclusion that might be drawn* . . . On the other hand, don't overdo the tentativeness by qualifying every statement you make. Consider three examples to illustrate the point:

TOO CONFIDENT: The study proves that schools are loosely-coupled systems.

TOO TENTATIVE: One conclusion that might be drawn from this study is that this particular school, on the basis of this investigation, seemed to have elements of organizational structure that might enable it to be characterized in general as a "loosely-coupled system," although there were clearly aspects of tight coupling manifest in certain parts of the system.

BETTER: The findings suggest that most of the organizational elements of this school were only loosely linked, so that it might be generally characterized as "loosely coupled."

And most of all, document your assertions. This matter is so important that perhaps it needs special examination.

Document Assertions

One mark of the scholarly paper is that assertions are documented; the writer provides evidence for statements that might be reasonably challenged. In contrast, the paper written for a mass audience or one written by a novice typically abounds in generalizations without evidence. The journalist writes: "Experts now believe that most large employers will soon be providing child-care services for working parents." The scholar writes: "According to several studies, a large percentage of the companies employing more than 1,000 employees provide some form of child care for working parents (see, for example, the Murphy 1997 survey)."

In writing a dissertation, documentation is essential, because the dissertation is scholarly in nature. This means that you should provide evidence for every general statement that is open to challenge.

There are three general approaches to handling this problem. One way, obviously, is to avoid it: Couch the observation in a way that does not require documentation. Contrast these two versions:

1. Schools are more and more getting back to the basics.
2. A reading of both professional journals and the popular press during the past few years would suggest strongly that many public school administrators and teachers are more concerned with what is loosely termed "the basics."

The first statement is open to challenge: Which schools? How many? Do you mean pupils, parents, teachers, or administrators? What evidence do you have? What basics? The statement requires either careful documentation or extensive revision. The second statement is more cautious and also more specific. It makes a general observation about how the popular and professional publications are concerned with the issue; it specifies "administrators and teachers" instead of the vague "schools"; it uses words like "would suggest" and "many" to indicate tentativeness; and it admits that there is some vagueness about the term "the basics." It is wordy—but it is a defensible assertion couched in a way that does not require documentation. A second choice is to offer in the text itself the evidence that supports the assertion. The following example illustrates this second choice: "There has been in recent years increased interest in cooperative learning among both researchers and practitioners. A survey of the entries in *Current Index to Journals in Education* for the years 1985-1995 indicates that . . . " Here you provide the evidence directly, noting the facts that support the general assertion.

The third and more commonly used option is to cite other sources that provide the evidence. You refer the reader to the literature that provides the support for the claim you make. Here is an example of this approach. "Several years ago, researchers turned their attention to interactive and recursive models of the composing process (see, for example, Graves, 1985; Applebee, 1987)."

In making citations to support assertions, you are expected to demonstrate scholarly integrity.

- Do not cite sources you have not read.
- Wherever possible, cite primary, not secondary, sources.
- Do not distort the source; don't twist the evidence just to support your own notions.

You can overdo the documentation, of course—but when in doubt, document.

Vary the Way You Identify Sources

There are several ways to cite sources. Suppose, for example, you wish to cite a 1998 study by Walker that concluded that parents reported satisfaction with the charter school their children attended. Here are several ways you can cite this source:

- According to Walker (1998), parents reported satisfaction . . .
- Walker (1998) concluded that . . .
- Parents reported a high level of satisfaction with the charter schools their children attended (Walker, 1998).
- Several studies conclude that parents are generally satisfied with the charter school their children attended (see, for example, Jones, 1996; King, 1990; Walker, 1998).
- In the 1998 study by Walker . . .

Vary the way you cite sources, to avoid excessive repetition.

Use Appropriate Paragraphing

The length and structure of the paragraph play an important part in the scholarly style. The length of a paragraph is primarily a factor of format and audience. An article printed in a journal with very narrow columns will tend to be divided into shorter paragraphs in order to increase readability; chapters in textbooks will tend to run longer, unless written for an immature audience. Shorter paragraphs are easier to read—or at least *look* easier to read; longer paragraphs seem more difficult. Besides factors of format and audience, the most important concern is for the way your ideas and information are segmented. Textbooks on writing usually advise that each paragraph should focus on one main idea. In general, that is good advice; all other things being equal, divide a paragraph when you think you have come to the end of an idea or set of information. A good rule of thumb to keep in mind in writing dissertations is this one: Write main paragraphs of about 100-150 words in length or longer. Very short paragraphs, as noted above, might give the impression of an immature style or shallow thinking; paragraphs that are too long do not invite the reader to read. Also, be sensitive to the norms of your own profession, because there seem to be differences here. Paragraphs in science reports, for example, tend to be shorter than those in education articles.

In terms of the structure of the paragraph, remember that paragraphs in scholarly writing tend to move from the general to the specific. You start the paragraph with a general statement and then provide the specifics to develop and support that general statement. Occasionally the order is reversed; the paragraph begins with specifics and ends with a generalization. Ordinarily, however, the general-to-specific pattern is easier for the reader to follow and understand.

Write Clear, Mature Sentences

It is not feasible in this book to present a full treatment of sentence structure and sentence effectiveness; instead, this discussion can only point to some general features of the scholarly sentence and offer some general points of advice. Readers interested in a more extensive treatment of the sentence should consult any handbook on writing style and usage; several excellent ones are available in the university bookstore. The discussion that follows concentrates on those issues that are most important in the dissertation.

1. *Combine shorter sentences.* Shorter sentences suggest immaturity. Consider these examples:

TOO SHORT: Gray (1998) studied the effectiveness of the new schedule. He used scores on the Stanford Achievement Test as the measure.

COMBINED: Gray (1998) studied the effectiveness of the new schedule, using scores on the Stanford Achievement Test as the measure.

2. *Put the main idea in the main clause.* The main clause is the part of the sentence that can stand by itself; it should contain the main idea. The mistake of putting the main idea in a subordinate structure is called "incorrect subordination." Here is an example:

INCORRECT: The schedule was in effect only 1 year, with students achieving better results.

BETTER: Students achieved better results, although the schedule was in effect only 1 year.

3. *Reduce the number of* ands. Excessive use of the conjunction *and* suggests a childish style. Consider these two examples:

TOO MANY *ANDS*: The teacher put the assignment on the board, and then she checked the roll and found that three students were absent.

BETTER: After putting the assignment on the board, the teacher found by checking the roll that three students were absent.

4. *Achieve an effect of clarity and directness by expressing the main action of the sentence in the verb and the main doer of the action (the agent) in the subject.* Scholarly writing especially suffers from the vagueness that comes from burying the action in a noun and using nonaction verbs like *do, make, have, be, perform,* and *occur.* Consider the following examples:

VAGUE AND WORDY: Orientations and explanations are important methods used by teachers in teaching writing.

BETTER: Teachers teach writing by orienting and explaining.

Words like *orientations* and *explanations* are called nominalizations. Nominalizations are nouns made from verbs: *orientation* from *orient, explanations* from *explain*. In general, avoid excessive nominalization.

5. *Avoid inserting long modifiers between the subject and the verb.* For the most part, a sentence is easier to read if the subject and verb are reasonably close. Consider these two examples:

TOO SEPARATED: School administrators who are interested in making changes that are not too expensive or too complex for the most part have been overly receptive to simplistic solutions.

BETTER: Because many school administrators seem interested in making only simple and inexpensive changes, they have been overly receptive to simplistic solutions.

6. *Avoid using subordinate clauses that modify other subordinate clauses.* This mistake is called "tandem subordination." It produces sentences like this one: "One of the obstacles that deter the installation of solar energy systems that are designed to achieve the savings that are important to all people is the reluctance of those same individuals to make large capital investments."

BETTER: Many people are reluctant to install solar energy systems because of the large capital investment required.

7. *Place modifiers so that they clearly modify what you intend them to modify.* As your tenth-grade English teacher reminded you, participles and reduced clauses are especially troublesome in this regard. Be sure that every such modifier clearly relates to the appropriate antecedent. Here are two examples to illustrate this point:

INCORRECT: Having explained the directions, the students began to write.

CORRECT: After the teacher explained the directions, the students began to write.

8. *Avoid excessive use of the passive voice.* In the passive voice, the receiver of the action is the subject and the doer is buried in a phrase, as in this example:

PASSIVE: The test was taken by the students.
ACTIVE: The students took the test.

The third-person passive voice was once considered desirable because it conveyed a detached, scholarly tone that hid the writer and seemed to connote objectivity. It also resulted in a wordy, lifeless style, as illustrated by this sentence: "It was decided by this researcher that the effects of socioeconomic status should be investigated as a factor that might possibly affect the amount of reading done in the home." This is more direct: "The researcher investigated the relationship between socioeconomic status and the amount of reading done at home."

One way of avoiding the excessive use of the passive is to use *I* to refer to the researcher, as in this example: "Next, I administered the test." The only caution here is the obvious one: Do not overdo it. Do not riddle your paper with *I*'s. You are writing a dissertation, not a personal essay. Also be sure to clear this approach with your chair.

9. *Be consistent in matters of verb tense.* This matter gets complicated. Here are some general rules that should work in most cases:

- Use future tense in the proposal. "A random sample of students will be selected . . ."
- Use past tense in the literature review, unless you are referring to a current belief of the researcher, as in these examples:

  Slavin (1990) determined that individual accountability . . .
  Slavin (1996) indicates that his comprehensive program . . .

- In the dissertation, use past tense for the design or procedure (e.g., "the sample was selected").
- In the dissertation, use present tense to describe and discuss the results that are there before the reader (e.g., "suggests that integrated programs . . . ").

Some Special Matters of Word Choice and Form

For specific advice about word choice and usage, you should refer to one of the good usage reference works readily available. Also,
of course, rely upon one of the standard style guides for matters of
form. Check with your chair to determine which style guide is required. If none is specified, use the current edition of the APA *Publication Manual.* It might be helpful, however, to note here a few specific matters that seem to cause special problems to writers of
dissertations. A summary of these specific issues is presented on the
following pages in Exhibit 12.3.

Grammar and Usage

1. Use jargon with discrimination. *Jargon* is the special language of your profession; it is so essential in discourse among professionals that you would have difficulty communicating clearly without it. Minimize your use of jargon and avoid terms that seem outdated and used too often.

2. Avoid fad expressions that have a brief vogue in your profession and then disappear. Most educators are tired of hearing about "paradigm shifts," for example.

3. Avoid colloquial expressions. Colloquial expressions such as *a lot, write up, tracked down, checked up on* seem out of place in a dissertation.

4. Avoid the use of contractions such as *it's, they're, didn't.* Their use is too colloquial.

5. Avoid adjectival nouns. English has a vital capacity for making adjectives out of nouns; consider, for example, such combinations as *steel door, school teacher, street sign.* Avoid such awkward combinations, however, as these: *achievement test data analysis, school administration theory studies, writer anxiety test results.*

6. Avoid the vague use of *we* and *our.* These pronouns are often ambiguous in terms of to whom they refer. Here is an example of ambiguous use: "We should be more concerned with student responsibility." This is a clearer version: "Educators should be more concerned with student responsibility."

7. Avoid the second-person *you* (and the imperative mode) unless you wish to communicate very directly with your readers. The imperative states a command or wish, without using the pronoun *you*: "Consider the next issue." Notice that this book makes extensive use of *you*—and the imperative mode—but this is not a research report.

8. Avoid the sexist use of the masculine pronoun in referring to males and females. Use the plural forms because they are not gender specific, or use a substitute such as *his or her.*

Exhibit 12.3. Specific Matters of Style

SEXIST: A teacher should avoid imposing his opinions on students.

BETTER: Teachers should avoid imposing their opinions on students.

9. The word *data* is usually considered plural. Say: "These data are . . . " Some dictionaries now note that the word is often used as a singular noun ("this data was . . . "), but the plural is probably safer.

Punctuation

10. The comma and the period always go inside the quotation mark. Here is an example of correct punctuation: "Although many researchers have analyzed organizations as 'loosely coupled systems,' only a few have bothered to define what is meant by 'loose coupling.'"

Direct Quotation and Paraphrase

11. Use direct quotation only when it is important to preserve the exact words of the original. In most cases, paraphrase.

Format

12. Avoid the use of boldface and italics. Use underlining where appropriate.

13. Use double spacing for the narrative. The APA *Publication Manual* recommends that you use single spacing for table titles and headings, figure captions, references (with double space between references), footnotes, and long quotations. That style manual also recommends using triple space after chapter titles, between major subheadings, and before and after tables in the text.

Use of Tables

14. Use tables to present complex data. In the text itself, refer the reader to the table, commenting on the highlights without simply repeating what is included in the table.

Exhibit 12.3. Continued

13

Organizing the Dissertation

How are dissertations organized? What principles govern the organization of individual chapters? How can the organization be made clear to the reader? And how is the dissertation finally packaged? These are all important issues that confront the doctoral student at the outset. This chapter will examine these questions in the order posed.

How Are Dissertations Organized?

The answer to this question is simple: in whatever way enables you to communicate your results clearly to the reader. Techniques of organization have no intrinsic value; they operate only to facilitate communication—to help you achieve your goal of informing the reader. Obviously, the particular organizational strategy you choose will be affected by such considerations as the nature of your study, the field in which you are working, and the particular requirements of your department.

There is a general pattern widely used in most dissertations, not just because it is sanctioned by tradition, but because it has its own internal logic. This pattern provides answers to five fundamental questions:

1. *What is the problem that I studied?* This typically is the concern of the first chapter. The specific content of that first chapter will be discussed more in detail below.

2. *How does my study relate to previous work?* This is the review of the literature, usually Chapter 2.

3. *What methods did I use to study the problem?* Chapter 3 typically is an explication of the methodology.

4. *What results did I obtain?* The reporting of the results might require more than one chapter.

5. *What does it all mean?* The dissertation ends with a summary and discussion of the results.

As noted above, there are many variations to this basic pattern. In some cases, you might feel that a review of the literature would be better integrated into the rest of the dissertation rather than standing as a separate chapter unto itself. In some dissertations, the methodology is so implicit in the nature of the inquiry that you might feel that no separate treatment is needed. Some faculties now require the student to produce a publishable article, instead of writing a standard dissertation.

To illustrate more clearly this notion that the organization of the dissertation can vary with the nature of the study, consider the following plan for a qualitative dissertation:

QUALITATIVE STUDY OF TEAM LEADERSHIP

Chapter 1. Introduction

Chapter 2. Methodology

Chapter 3. Phase 1: Eager decision making

Chapter 4. Phase 2: Conflict and dissonance

Chapter 5. Phase 3: Becoming a mature team

Chapter 6. Summary and discussion

Rather than writing a separate chapter reviewing the literature, the student decided, with the approval of the chair, to integrate the literature review wherever appropriate.

If you feel at all uncertain about the best order, stand back from your study, consider your readers, work out a tentative plan for the order of chapters, and check with your chair.

What Principles Govern
the Organization of Individual Chapters?

First, each chapter must seem to relate to the whole. The reader should have the feeling that he or she is reading a unified narrative, not a collection of individual pieces. Next, each chapter should make sense by itself and be organized in such a way that the reader can easily follow the line of argument. Finally, the parts of the chapter should clearly relate to each other, conveying a sense of order and form. Also, be sure to frame each chapter with a definite introduction that opens the chapter and suggests what is to come and a clear conclusion that draws the chapter to a close.

The organizational patterns found in most dissertations are summarized in Exhibit 13.1. The suggestions presented in Exhibit 13.1 are not intended as a rigid formula. They are offered only as typical patterns. If they seem useful to you with your dissertation, use them. However, be sure that each chapter has its own sense of order.

How Can the Organization
Be Made Clear to the Reader?

This is an important issue, for if the organization is clear only to you, then you have failed in communicating with the reader. You have an obligation to make your plan clear, to provide the reader with a verbal road map, so that the journey is made without detours. It is probably wiser to err on the side of overemphasizing the plan. Readers will forgive you more readily for providing too many maps than they will for confusing them.

You begin by indicating in Chapter 1 how the dissertation is organized. You open each chapter by linking it with the previous chapter and by indicating what will come. In these ways you provide the reader with an overall framework for the dissertation. Then, as explained in Chapter 12, you use headings and subheadings at the major divisions of the chapter. As each division begins, you use a transition paragraph or a transition sentence to show the connection between that division and what has gone before. A transition paragraph is a short paragraph that links major sections of the paper. The first sentence looks back to the previous section or division.

Chapter and Emphasis	Typical Pattern
1. Statement of the problem	a. General background of the study b. Problem statement c. Professional significance of the problem d. Overview of the methodology e. Delimitations of the study f. Definitions of key terms g. Organization of the dissertation
2. A review of the literature	a. An overview of how the chapter is organized b. Review of the theoretical and empirical literature, organized according to one of certain patterns c. A summary of what the previous research seems to mean and how it relates to this study
3. The methodology of the study	a. A description of the general methodology b. The research context or site c. The subjects or participants d. The instruments and materials used e. The procedures followed f. The data analyses made g. A summary statement of the methodology
4. The results of the study	a. An overview of the chapter b. A presentation of the results, organized in terms of how the problem statement was posed in the first chapter c. A summary in general terms of the results obtained
5. The summary and discussion	a. A summary of the results, organized in terms of how the problem statement was posed b. A discussion of the findings

Exhibit 13.1. Typical Organizational Pattern

The second sentence looks ahead. A transition sentence has the same structure in condensed form: The first part of the sentence, usually a subordinate clause, looks back. The second part, usually the main clause, looks ahead.

Following is an example from the dissertation on student questions. Assume that the writer has just finished writing the section on types of student questions. Here is the transition that might be used to lead into the next section on frequency of student questions: "In addition to this examination of the types of questions, researchers have also studied the frequency of question asking." Notice that the first part of the sentence looks back and the second part looks ahead.

You also use paragraphing effectively as an aid to organization. Do not begin and end paragraphs whimsically, when the spirit moves you. End a paragraph when you have fully developed an idea. Then begin a new one when you are ready to move to a new idea. Keep in mind the caution noted in Chapter 12: Dissertations call for longer paragraphs. The longer paragraph suggests seriousness, formality, scholarship, and depth. Aim for a 100-word minimum. That seems arbitrary, of course. The point is that much shorter paragraphs will seem superficial.

Consider also the use of topic sentences as aids to organizational clarity. The topic sentence is a sentence that states the main idea of the paragraph. Topic sentences usually come first in expository prose, when they are used. Professional writers do not use or think about topic sentences. However, they are of help to the writer learning the craft. They give a shape to the paragraph, and they aid the reader. They say very clearly, "This is what this paragraph is about."

Here is an example of a topic sentence that ties the rest of the paragraph together: "Most of the research on the relationship of subject to frequency of student questions has concluded that students ask more questions in mathematics class than they do in other subjects. Morris (1995) determined that middle school students in mathematics classes . . . "

At the beginning of paragraphs and within the paragraph, make appropriate use of transition devices. A transition device is any expression or verbal strategy that helps the reader make connections. These are the devices most typically used:

1. Using a counting word—*first, second, next, finally.*
2. Using an expression that shows the relationship of ideas—*on the other hand, however, as a result, furthermore, consequently,* etc.
3. Repeating a key word, as in this example: "Middle school students seem to ask more questions than high school students.

These *middle school students,* according to Meiser (1993), seem less inhibited in their questioning behavior."

4. Using a pronoun that refers to a key term, as in this example: "Questions of diversion are intended to lead the teacher from the topic at hand. *They* seem to lighten the classroom climate."

Excessive use of such transition devices can seem heavy-handed. It may make more sense if you think about a basic matter of raising and meeting expectations. Scholars who have studied coherence in English have pointed out that coherence, the quality of seeming to stick together, really seems to emerge when the writer first raises certain expectations in the reader and then meets those expectations. Writing that seems disconnected either is not clear about the expectations or fails to meet the expectations raised.

Perhaps that basic notion sums up all this advice about organization: Make clear to the reader what you plan to do—and then keep that bargain, clarifying how you have kept it.

How Is the Dissertation Finally Packaged?

The order and appearance of the final dissertation package are important matters: Check with your adviser about special requirements of your school and consult whatever style manual is recommended. A standard order is presented below, with some brief comments where appropriate. (See Chapter 19 for additional details.)

Abstract. Remember that the abstract will probably appear by itself in one of the retrieval services. Be sure it reads well, describes your study accurately, and seems self-contained. State the problem clearly, indicate briefly the methodology used, summarize the results, and comment briefly about their implications. Do not include any bibliographic references, tables, figures, abbreviations, or acronyms. Abstracts submitted to University Microfilms International must not exceed 350 words.

Title page. In choosing a title, remember that it should be brief, descriptive, and clear. In thinking of a good title, ask yourself this question: "If I were another reader trying to find this study, what key terms would I look for?" The answer should indicate to you what terms are important to include. Do not include phrases like *a study of* or *an investigation of.* Also keep in mind the scholarly impact of using a colon in your title: Many scholarly books, articles, and dissertations use a colon in the title. Here are two examples to illustrate these points.

> POOR TITLE: A Qualitative Study of How Teacher Leaders Actually Function in a Site-Based Management School
>
> BETTER TITLE: Teacher Leadership: New Roles in Site-Based Management

Approval page. In some institutions, the approval of the committee and the dean is indicated on the title page; in others, a separate page is included.

Acknowledgments page. Most dissertations include an acknowledgments page in which the writer acknowledges the assistance received. It is expected that you will acknowledge the assistance of the committee, paying special tribute to the role the adviser played. You also should acknowledge any special financial support from funding agencies. You should note any editorial help you have received. If you wish, you also may acknowledge the assistance of a long-suffering spouse. But keep this section brief—and don't be too effusive.

Contents. Call the page *Contents,* not *Table of Contents.*

List of tables and figures.

The chapters. Present them in the order you think is clearest.

References. Most dissertations end with a list of references, with only works cited in the dissertation itself.

Appendixes. Include in the appendix section any supporting material that does not seem to belong in the main body of the dissertation.

Some universities expect an index to be included; check on your university's requirements here.

14

Writing the Introductory Chapter

The first chapter seems to present special problems to writers of dissertations. Perhaps it is the realization that finally they have to begin. Perhaps it is the fear of making a false start. More likely, it is the problem of simply not knowing how to start. What do you include in the first chapter—and in what order?

To a certain extent, of course, the answers to those questions are determined by the type of research and the nature of the dissertation. The best way to learn how to write the first chapter of your dissertation is to read other dissertations similar to yours. You should also discuss the matter with your chair.

However, there is one general pattern that seems to work for most dissertations. It goes like this:

- Introduction to the chapter
- Background of the study
- The problem statement
- The professional significance of the study
- Overview of methodology
- Delimitations of the study
- Definitions of key terms

The remainder of this chapter examines each of these components.

Introduction to the Chapter

The main function of this opening section is simply to get the reader into the chapter somewhat gradually, rather than jumping directly into the first substantive division. It can be as brief as one paragraph; it can be as long as three or more pages. If you prefer a briefer introduction, then begin with a paragraph something like this:

> This dissertation is a report of an ethnographic study of the teaching of writing. The study was based primarily upon the direct observation of a fifth-grade teacher in an urban school district who used an "experience" approach to the teaching of language arts. This first chapter of the dissertation presents the background of the study, specifies the problem of the study, describes its significance, and presents an overview of the methodology used. The chapter concludes by noting the delimitations of the study and defining some special terms used.

A paragraph of this sort is very direct and to the point: It states the problem of the research and tells the reader what to expect in the rest of the chapter.

If you do not like such a direct beginning, then start with a more discursive and reflective opening. You might note the special professional conditions at the time of your study, you might reflect a bit on the broad concern your study addresses, or you might refer to the societal conditions that made the problem seem important. Here's an example of a somewhat more discursive opening paragraph:

> The quest for a better reading program is one of those beguiling challenges that continue to intrigue educators even in a time characterized by cynicism about educational innovation. Even after decades of unproductive experimentation, scholars and educational leaders still search for the optimal curricular and instructional approach that will solve once and for all "the reading problem." And teachers implement whatever new approach seems to promise amelioration, as long as that new approach is not too discrepant with present practice.

The writer would then continue to comment on the search for a better program and slowly lead into the problem of the study: how a classroom teacher implements a new reading program.

1. Introduction to the Study

This dissertation is a report of an ethnographic study of the teaching of writing. The study was based primarily upon the direct observation of a fifth-grade teacher in an urban school district who . . .

Background of the Study

It might be useful at this juncture to describe briefly the professional developments occurring at the time that influenced the study. It was first of all a time when the public in general and . . .

Exhibit 14.1. Example of Introductory Chapter

Note two matters of style here. First, in referring to your study in this and subsequent chapters, use the past tense: Write as if the study is concluded, even though it might not be when you are writing the first chapter. For example, "This study examined . . . " Second, the introduction to the chapter does not have its own heading. The first page of Chapter 1 looks like the one shown in Exhibit 14.1. (Throughout this work, all exhibit headings are handled in the style recommended by the APA *Publication Manual,* 4th Edition; check your own style guide for variations.)

The Background of the Study

This section is intended to provide a context for your study. It answers the question "What special factors were at work that might possibly have influenced the conceptualization and execution of the study?" Ordinarily the "background" section will take only 2-5 pages, again depending upon the nature of your study and your own approach to writing. In this section you might deal with such special background factors as the following:

- *The societal background*: developments and changes in the society that made the problem seem important
- *The intellectual background*: major intellectual and philosophical movements of the time that provided a special context for the study
- *The professional background*: developments in your field that made the problem seem worth studying
- *The research background*: new methods that seemed worth using or new theories that seemed to need testing; gaps in existing knowledge

Ordinarily, personal factors are considered irrelevant in the dissertation; the dissertation is a scholarly report, and readers typically are not interested in you as the researcher. Also, local factors are typically not identified. The fact that your school district needed a new teacher evaluation system is not worth mentioning in a dissertation that you hope will have a much broader impact.

The Problem Statement

The problem statement is a very brief section, perhaps only one-half page, in which you state the problem as clearly as possible. Though brief, it is a crucial section, since the way you state the problem will directly influence the way you present and summarize the results. The way the problem is stated will vary with the nature of the study. Review the problem statement forms explained previously in Chapter 10.

The Professional Significance of the Study

With the problem stated, you turn next to the section concerned with the significance of the study. Your purpose here is simple: to answer the question "Why did you bother to conduct the study?" In answering this question, your tone is important. You do not want to claim too much. Statements of this sort make readers bristle: "No other issue is more critical in the field of education today." You also need to be rather specific about the need or the significance, indicating by a careful analysis that the study is important from more than one point of view. Here are some of the ways in which you can argue for the study:

1. The general problem has intrinsic importance, affecting organizations or people.
2. Previous studies have turned up conflicting evidence concerning the specific issue that you have chosen to study.
3. Your study examines in a real-life setting the implementation of a program based on a theory that has been widely accepted but little tested.
4. The study is such that any meaningful results would seem to be of value to practitioners.
5. The population or the setting chosen is sufficiently unique that the study seems likely to advance knowledge in the field.
6. The methods you have chosen for the study have not been widely used in your profession, and your study will likely yield some useful methodological findings.

Notice that in each case you argue from a broad perspective; you do not claim significance by asserting that your organization benefited.

Overview of Methodology

The next questions that you should answer are, "How did you conduct the study? Which method did you use?" These questions will be answered fully in the chapter on methodology, probably, but it seems useful to include in the first chapter a general statement of the method used in order to round out the introductory picture presented to the reader. Ordinarily, a page or two of general discussion of methodology will be appropriate; be sure, of course, that you note that the issue is fully discussed at a later point in the dissertation. In your general discussion of methodology, you should note the research perspective, the research type, and the research methods in brief.

Delimitations

You also may wish to include a separate section that notes the delimitations of the study. Students often misunderstand the special research meaning of *delimitations*; it does not mean "flaws" or "weaknesses." Such an interpretation results in an apology for the study that prejudices the reader against the study at the very outset. Instead, the term should be construed as having two other related denotations: the boundaries of the study, and ways in which the findings may lack generalizability. In considering this matter of delimitations, you would examine such concerns as the nature and size of the sample, the uniqueness of the setting, the time period during which the study was conducted, and the limitations of the particular methods selected.

Definitions of Key Terms

Most introductory chapters probably should include definitions of special terms used in the study. Do not feel obligated to define terms that are generally understood by those in your profession. You should, instead, ordinarily include definitions only when one or more of these conditions obtains:

- The term is relatively new in your profession and has not gained general currency.
- The term is often used ambiguously in the profession, and you wish to give it some preciseness.
- The term is a general one, and you wish to use it in a rather special way.

Definitions are expected to be written according to a somewhat standardized pattern. You first state the term. Then you identify the broad class to which the term belongs, using the same part of speech as the term itself. Then you specify the particular ways in which that term differs from others in its class. Here's an example:

> *Alternative school*: a public (not private or independent) school whose program is considered to be substantially different from standard educational programs and which students choose to attend rather than attending the school to which they would ordinarily be assigned.

Observe that the general class is identified: a public school. The term being identified is next distinguished parenthetically from other classes (not private or independent), and then the two important distinguishing features are noted.

In considering the matter of definitions, you might wish to keep in mind a distinction between "system languages" (the special terms and meanings used in a given scholarly discipline) and "common language" (the words and meanings used in everyday discourse). This distinction means that you should not invent new words when the existing system language is adequate. Also, keep in mind that words that have a special system meaning should not be used to denote their common language meaning. For example, the word *significant* should not be used to mean "important" in a dissertation that will also use the term in its system sense of "having statistical significance."

The first chapter probably should conclude with a paragraph that looks ahead to the rest of the dissertation, indicating to readers what they may expect. Such a conclusion is not obligatory, but some general type of ending is expected by the reader. Write a few sentences that say to the reader, "This chapter is finished; prepare for the next one." Keep in mind, finally, that these suggestions about the opening chapter describe a general pattern that seems to work. Check with your dissertation adviser or your department about any special requirements or formats.

15

Writing the Review
of the Literature

The review of the literature is provided in a dissertation for a very specific reason. It presents to the reader the knowledge base upon which your study is built. This purpose reflects a time-honored tradition of scientific research: It acknowledges its indebtedness to the past and shows clear linkages between what was known in the past about the topic and what was discovered in the present research. This chapter will explain one process you can use in writing an effective review of the literature.

As explained in previous chapters, the review of the literature usually constitutes Chapter 2 of the dissertation. In a small number of graduate schools, however, the student is encouraged to integrate the references to the literature throughout the dissertation, wherever appropriate, rather than writing a separate chapter. Be sure to check with your dissertation chair at the proposal defense. The following discussion assumes that you will have to write a separate chapter.

Update the Comprehensive Critique of the Literature

The first step is to update your comprehensive critique of the literature. You want to be sure that your review is as current as you can make it. You should therefore do one more search of ERIC, requesting the most recent sources. You should check current issues of journals that publish educational research. You should use the Internet to contact other researchers working in your general field of study. You also should attend scholarly conferences and check conference programs so that you can send for papers that might not yet be published or entered into computerized databases.

Reread All Sources

The next step is to reread all the usable sources that you have located. The purpose of this rereading is to freshen your understanding of what has been learned about the topic of your study. There are several systematic ways you can complete the rereading; the following method has worked effectively for many students. To clarify the process, the discussion assumes that the researcher is writing a review of the research on teachers' professional development.

1. *Review each topical file.* If you have followed the process explained in previous chapters, you have copies of all the sources filed in folders arranged topically. Take the first file and arrange the sources in order by date of publication. In the example used here, the first topical file might be "Stages of teachers' career development."

2. *Identify each source with an appropriate code number to simplify the way you refer to it in your own work.* Thus, in the example used here, you might code the first article "Career stages 1."

3. *Cross-reference sources appropriately.* If one of the sources in a given topical file contains material on another topic, make a simple notecard for the second topical file, reminding you of the source you should check. Suppose, for example, that the source "Career stages 1," which discusses "stages of teachers' career development," also contains usable material on "fostering teachers' development"; you would then make a notecard reading "See Career stages 1" and add it to the "fostering" folder.

4. *Reread each source and write a brief summary of it to remind you of its main points and its perceived value to your review.* Here is an example: "Stages 7. Huberman identifies 5 stages, each with a different theme. In stages 3 and 4, the teacher may take one of two paths. Very useful review." Clip the summary to the source.

In this rereading process, put aside the following types of sources: opinions about current educational issues; reports of practice; and prescriptions of what should be done. Unless your chair advises you to the contrary, you should include only the theoretical literature and the empirical research.

Develop the Final Outline

You should now be ready to develop the final outline. You probably have your own method of outlining. The following process has worked well for many student researchers.

Determine the Major Components of the Chapter

The first step in outlining involves the identification of the major components of the literature review. You have several choices here, depending upon your own preferences and the requirements of the committee. Some reviews include an explanation of the search process that was used in assembling the review. Some reviews include a discussion of the theoretical literature. All include a review of the empirical research. Thus, there are four patterns frequently used.

Pattern 1

> The search process
> The theoretical literature
> The empirical research

Pattern 2

> The search process
> The empirical research

Pattern 3

> The theoretical literature
> The empirical research

Pattern 4

> The empirical research

As explained earlier, this matter should be resolved at the proposal defense, but you should check again as you get ready to write the chapter.

Analyze the Major Components Into Divisions and Subdivisions

Now take each major component and analyze it first into its own divisions. You do this by reflecting about this question: What are the big pieces of this component? If you have made wise choices in the way you have structured your files, then the way the files are organized can simplify this task for you. Here, for example, is how the researcher might identify the divisions of the component "methods of fostering teachers' professional development":

1. Supervision
2. Staff development
3. Graduate study
4. External workshops
5. Change in role
6. Change in teaching assignment

For divisions that are both complex and critical to the review, you may wish to note their subdivisions. In the example given above, the division *Supervision* might be further analyzed in this manner:

1. Supervision
   a. Standard approaches
   b. Innovative approaches

Develop and Submit the Final Outline

The steps explained above should prepare you to write the final outline. Exhibit 15.1 shows the final outline for the review of the literature on teachers' professional development.

Be sure to submit the final outline to your chair for his or her critique. You will spend a great deal of time writing the chapter, and you want to be sure that your time has not been wasted.

I. Search Process

II. Theoretical Literature

    A. Jackson

    B. Burden

    C. Huberman

III. Empirical Research

    A. Stages

        1. Entry

        2. Stabilization

        3. Experimentation/reassessment

        4. Serenity/conservatism

        5. Disengagement

    B. Factors influencing development

        1. Personal

        2. Contextual

        3. Intervention-related

    C. Means of fostering professional development

        1. Supervision

        2. Staff development

        3. Graduate study

        4. External workshops

        5. Change in role

        6. Change in teaching assignment

Exhibit 15.1. Outline, Teachers' Professional Development

Use Levels of Headings That Reflect the Outline

In all chapters, but especially in the review of the literature, use different levels of headings to reflect the outline and make clear to

[Level 1]   2. Review of the Literature

[Intro]   A large body of literature on the nature of teachers'

professional development provides a basis for the present

study. This chapter will explain the search process in reviewing

that literature and then examine both the theoretical and

empirical studies in the field.

[Level 2]   <u>Search Process</u>

The following review was developed through a systematic . . .

[Level 2]   <u>Theoretical Literature</u>

Several theories have been advanced to explain the nature . . .

[Level 2]   <u>Empirical Research</u>

The empirical studies that have been conducted have focused

on three elements: the stages of development; factors influ-

encing development; and means of fostering that development.

[Level 3] <u>Stages of Development</u>

Several major studies have examined teachers' professional

development through the several stages of growth.

[Level 4]   <u>Entry stage.</u> The entry stage, when the teachers begin their

careers, is chiefly a time when the teacher develops survival

skills.

Exhibit 15.2. Headings, Teachers' Professional Development the reader how the chapter is organized. In most dissertations, four levels should be sufficient for clarity, without getting too complex. Exhibit 15.2 shows how the four levels of headings can be used to reflect the outline shown in Exhibit 15.1; the heading style follows the recommendations of the APA *Publication Manual* (4th ed.). The title of the chapter is considered Level 1; the main divisions of the chapter, Level 2; subdivisions, Level 3; and sub-subdivisions, Level 4.

Write the Introductory Paragraph

The next step is to write the introduction to the chapter. Notice in Exhibit 15.2 that the introduction does not have its own heading. The introduction should be relatively brief, simply providing an overview of the chapter.

Write the First Section of the Review

Now you should turn to the first section. In the first and all succeeding sections, use this pattern: Provide an overview; generalize; specify.

Provide an Overview

Begin the first section with a brief overview, as shown in the first paragraph of Resource 15A. (Resource 15A will be used to illustrate several of the points that follow.) The overview helps the reader understand how that section is organized and what its main divisions are.

Generalize

Next, write the main developmental paragraphs of that section. Ordinarily, you should begin the developmental paragraphs with one or two sentences that generalize what the studies show, as Resource 15A indicates. Less-skilled writers simply enumerate the conclusions of each study, something like this: "Jones (1995) concluded that staff development programs are not effective. Joyce (1997) concluded that they can be effective if certain conditions hold true. Glickman (1998) concluded that coaching was an important condition of all successful programs." The point being made here is that you have an obligation to the reader to make coherent sense of the literature, instead of simply describing it.

Specify

With the generalization made, you next provide the specific evidence, citing and discussing each study relating to that generalization. How much space you devote to each study depends upon its importance. A major study should be treated at length, requiring one to four manuscript pages; a study of moderate significance for your own research needs only several paragraphs. A less-important study might simply be noted as one of several sources or be discussed briefly in one paragraph. Just be sure that the length of treatment corresponds to importance.

Write the Remaining Sections, Including a Summary

Use the same pattern of providing an overview, generalizing, and specifying in writing the remainder of the sections. Conclude the chapter with a summary, probably a page or two in length, that reviews the content of the chapter and brings together the key conclusions of all the empirical research.

Some Specific Reminders

As you write the chapter, keep in mind some specific suggestions made previously.

- Vary the way you refer to studies. Notice in the example in Resource 15A that the author uses several techniques.
- Paraphrase; do not quote. Quote directly only when it seems important to preserve the words of the original.
- Be sure each section is organized clearly, and give the reader verbal signals to indicate organization.
- Use headings that reveal the organizational pattern.

Is the review

1. Comprehensive, including all major works relating to your topic?

2. In-depth, providing the reader depth of knowledge about the prior research?

3. Current, including works published recently?

4. Selective, discriminating between major and less important studies?

5. Unbiased, without the writer skewing the prior research to suit his or her point of view?

6. Clearly organized, so that the reader can easily follow the plan and flow of the chapter?

7. Coherent, making sense of the studies, not simply describing them?

8. Effectively written, with a scholarly style?

Exhibit 15.3. Criteria: Literature Review

Evaluate and Revise

When you have finished writing the chapter, put it aside for a while. Then revise it, using such technological aids as a spell-check, a thesaurus, and a style-checker. You should also find the criteria listed in Exhibit 15.3 helpful in the revision process.

Resource 15A: Example of a Review Style

Factors Influencing Teachers' Professional Development

Three groups of factors seem to influence teacher development:

those involving the teacher as a person, those relating to the context,

and those involving specific interventions. Those three factors interact in a complex manner, affecting each other and in turn influencing teacher development.

Personal Factors

Several personal elements seem to exercise a critical influence in the teacher's professional growth. Most researchers who have examined these personal elements have taken a developmental perspective on such aspects as the following: chronological age, ego development, moral development, career development, cognitive development, and motivational development (see Burden, 1990, for a useful review). Of all these personal factors, the ones that seem to play the most significant role are the teacher's cognitive development, career development, and motivational development. The research on these three factors will be discussed in the following sections.

Cognitive development. The teacher's cognitive development is usually equated with the extent to which the teacher can reason conceptually. Building upon David Hunt's work in conceptual development, Glickman (1981) posited three levels of abstract thinking—low, moderate, and high. Teachers at a low level think more concretely, differentiate fewer concepts, and tend to see problems simplistically; those at a high level can reason abstractly, see connections between disparate elements, and enjoy complexity. Studies using conceptual level as the variable have concluded the following about teachers at the high level (as contrasted with those at the low level): They are more adaptable and flexible in teaching style, are more empathetic, provide more varied learning environments, are more tolerant of stress, are more effective with students of diverse ethnic backgrounds, and prefer to learn through a discovery model.

Although it would seem that cognitive level would be difficult to change, Sprinthall and Thies-Sprinthall (1983) provide evidence that cognitive development can be facilitated by placing persons in significant role-taking situations (such as mentoring), along with delivering continuous guided reflection and ongoing support.

Glickman's "developmental supervision" theory holds that supervisors working with teachers at a low level of conceptual development should be directive in their approach; with those at a moderate level, collaborative; and with those at a high level, nondirective. The research testing the effectiveness of such matching models seems inconclusive.

Career development. The term *career development* is used here to denote the growth experienced as teachers move through the stages of their professional careers. Several researchers have investigated the patterns of growth and stagnation that emerge as teachers re-main in the profession, each using different terms to identify the stages. The conceptualization that seems to be the most rigorous in its formulation is that advanced by Huberman (1989) (see Huber-man's 1989 article for a summary of the research).

Huberman's synthesis of the theory and research on career de-velopment posits five stages of the professional career, demarcated in terms of years of teaching experience. *Career entry,* from the first to the third year, is a time of both survival and discovery. The sur-vival theme is the one most often sounded in studies of beginning teachers; at the same time, many report a sense of discovery, as they work with their own pupils and become part of a collegial group. Those with from 4 to 6 years of teaching experience seem then to move into a *stabilization* period, when tenure is granted, a definitive commitment to the career of teaching is made, and a sense of in-structional mastery is achieved. Those with 7 to 18 years of experi-ence seem to diverge. Some teachers report this period as one of ex-perimentation and activism, when they try out new approaches, develop their own courses, and confront institutional barriers. Other teachers report this period as one of self-doubt and reassessment, when disenchantment with the system leads many to consider changing professions.

Divergence also occurs during the period of 19 to 30 years of experience. For many, it is a time of relaxed self-acceptance and serenity, accompanied by a developing awareness of greater relational distance from their pupils. For many other teachers, this period is one of conservatism; these teachers seem to complain a great deal, criticizing the administrators, their colleagues, and their students. The final period, from 31 to 40 years of teaching experience, is a stage of disengagement, a gradual withdrawal as the end of the career looms. For some, it is a time of serenity; for others, a time of bitterness.

Level of motivation. The third personal factor is the teacher's level of motivation—defined here as the strength of the inner drive to achieve professional goals. Glatthorn (1990) has identified several factors that, according to a significant body of research, influence the teacher's motivational level. The first is a supportive environment, which includes five features: Relationships with students and parents are positive, effective leadership is present, the physical conditions are adequate, the school climate is positive, and the teacher has a manageable teaching assignment. The second motivating factor is

meaningful work: The teacher has an appropriate degree of autonomy, and the teacher believes in the significance of the work.

The third factor is the teacher's belief system. The following beliefs are essential for a high level of motivation: I can perform successfully; the actions I take will achieve the results I want; those results will be recognized by rewards that I value. The fourth factor in
motivation is the teacher's goals. The teacher's level of motivation is
more likely to be high when the teacher's goals are shared by peers,
the goal-setting process is a collaborative one, the goals are specific,
and the goals are challenging but attainable.

Next, the rewards are significant. A teacher's level of motivation
is more likely to increase when more emphasis is placed on such intrinsic rewards as a sense of competence and a feeling of accom-
plishment and when student achievement is emphasized as a meaningful reward. The research in general concludes that teachers are
more motivated by such intrinsic rewards as the satisfaction of im-
proving learning than they are by such extrinsic ones as merit pay
(Dilworth, 1991). It should be noted here, however, that there may
be some national differences in the power of intrinsic elements. A
comparison of the attitudes of teachers in France and England concluded that inner-city French teachers are much less likely to per-

ceive teaching as a means of giving meaning to life and are far more likely to see it simply as a means of earning a living (Broadfoot & Osborn, 1987).

The final factor in teacher motivation is the type and frequency of feedback. Several studies suggest that the teacher's level of motivation is more likely to increase when the teacher makes continuing assessments of student learning and uses positive results as reinforcement. Additionally, frequent and positive feedback from administrators and supervisors can also increase the level of teacher motivation.

Contextual Factors

The contextual factors, as construed here, are all those elements of the environment that affect teacher development. The context is perceived broadly, as including what McLaughlin and Talbert (1990) term five embedded contextual layers. . . .

16

Explaining the Methodology

You should be able to write the methodology chapter without a great deal of difficulty if you have kept careful records. This chapter will explain what steps to take and what content to include in this chapter.

Prepare to Write the Chapter

In preparing to write the chapter, you can take several steps. First, you should reread Chapters 4 and 9 of this work. They both provide some helpful suggestions about the methodology. Second, review your records. Your researcher's journal should be especially useful. Finally, review your results; they will remind you of what methods you have used.

Use an Objective Style in Writing the Chapter

Objectivity is especially important in this chapter. In describing the research site, avoid making unsupported judgments, sweeping generalizations, and extreme statements. Instead, provide specific data, noting just the facts as you recorded them. Contrast these two versions:

TOO SUBJECTIVE: The school building looked as if a disaster had hit it. Nobody cared about the place or wanted to improve it. It was a terrible environment for learning.

MORE OBJECTIVE: The overall appearance of the building suggested that it was not well-maintained. Custodian Walker (a fictitious name) apologized for the appearance, noting that his staff had been cut. He noted that in early October he had reported to the head of facilities that the roof of the gym leaked, but by March when this study took place, nothing had been done.

To achieve specificity and objectivity, you may find it helpful to present much of the data in table form. If you do, be sure to use the format specified by your style guide. Remember that the table is used to present data, with the accompanying text used to comment on the highlights, not simply repeat what is in the table.

Determine the Content of the Chapter

With these preparatory steps accomplished, you should turn next to developing an outline of the chapter. To do so, you first need to determine the content of the chapter. Obviously, this will vary with the methods you have used and the steps you have taken. Most descriptions of methodology will include the following content: the general research perspective and research type; the research context, including a specification of time and place; the research participants; the instruments used in data collection; the procedures used in collecting the data; and the way you analyzed the data. A chapter summary is also typically included.

Outline the Chapter and Use Headings Appropriately

Now you are ready to develop the outline itself and use the outline to determine the headings you will use.

Make an Outline

After you have decided on content, you next should determine the overall organizational pattern. Four patterns are commonly found in dissertations, as follows.

Logical order. Most chapters will use a logical order, organizing the content in terms of the relationships of the concepts. Such an order

3. Methodology

This chapter explains the methods used in carrying out the study, giving special emphasis to the analysis of data. It should be noted at the outset that the methodology was to a certain extent an evolving one that took definite shape as the study progressed.

The General Perspective

As a qualitative study, the research reported here embodied both a quantitative and a qualitative perspective . . .

The Research Context

The study took place in a charter school in its first year of operation. For purposes of confidentiality, the school will be referred to with the fictitious name . . .

The Research Participants

Although the researcher was inevitably aware of the actions of both the director and the students, his primary concern was with the actions of the teachers . . .

Instruments Used in Data Collection

Several instruments and recording processes were used in the data collection process. First, . . .

Procedures Used

In carrying out the research design, several specific procedures were used . . .

Exhibit 16.1. Example of Methodology Chapter

<u>Data Analysis</u>

The data were analyzed using several strategies. First, the data were reduced by . . .

<u>Summary of the Methodology</u>

To summarize the previous explanation, it should be emphasized that the study used both . . .

Exhibit 16.1. Continued

is shown in Exhibit 16.1. You reflect about the processes you used and determine how best to group them. The logical order shown in Exhibit 16.1 will be used to organize the discussion that follows, because it includes most of the elements included in the methodology chapter.

Chronological order. Some researchers using a qualitative or action research approach prefer to follow a chronological order, discussing the steps in the order in which they were taken. This pattern is especially useful when the sequence of steps makes a difference.

Research questions order. Another organizational pattern frequently used in dissertations is to explain the methodology in relation to the research questions answered. Consider the following example (the researcher studying teachers' planning as it related to curriculum standards posed these three specific questions):

Question 1. To what extent are teachers familiar with curriculum standards?

Question 2. To what extent do teachers use curriculum standards in making yearly plans?

Question 3. To what extent are teachers conscious of using curriculum standards as they teach?

1. General research perspective and type

2. Research context and participants

3. Methods used for Question 1

4. Methods used for Question 2

5. Methods used for Question 3

6. Summary

Exhibit 16.2. Outline by Question

The researcher used those three questions to organize the methodology chapter, using the simple outline shown in Exhibit 16.2.

Research methods order. Finally, you may find that organizing the chapter in relation to the research methods makes most sense. Thus, you might have sections identified as follows: observation methods, interview methods, and survey methods.

Common elements. Regardless of the organizational pattern used, two initial elements are common to most dissertations: the general perspective and the research context. The reader would also expect to find an introductory paragraph and a summary.

Once you have developed an outline, submit it to your chair for review.

Use Appropriate Headings

After the chair has approved the outline, be sure to use headings that will reflect it and make it clear to the reader. Note that the headings shown in Exhibit 16.1 use only Level 1 for the chapter title and Level 2 for the main divisions. You may need to use Level 3 to identify subdivisions of the Level 2 headings.

Describe the Context of the Study

The term *context* is used to identify the place and time of the study. A detailed description of the research site will enable other researchers and readers to better understand the findings. Depending on the nature of your study, you can choose to describe one or more of the following levels:

- State department and the regional service center
- School district or school system
- School
- Classroom or other special location
- Community

Which aspects do you include in your description? The answer is all those that the reader needs to understand the specialness of the research context. Exhibit 16.3 lists most of the aspects that might be included for school district, school, classroom, and community—the contexts most often used in educational research. Do not use that list as a prescription; use it instead as a set of guidelines designed to help you decide what to include.

In most dissertations, you should give these entities fictitious names in order to preserve confidentiality. Indicate that the name is fictitious the first time you use it. This is one way you can do so: "Lincoln High School is a large Grades 9-12 high school in a major city in the East. (Lincoln is a fictitious name, used to preserve confidentiality.)"

In describing the context, be sure to indicate as well the time period for the study, perhaps in this manner: "The research activities covered a 2-month period, from March 1, 1999, to May 30, 1999."

Identify the Subjects or Participants

You also need to provide specific information about all those who participated in the study. In most quantitative studies they are identified as *subjects*; in most qualitative studies, as *participants*. In either case, provide the specific information the reader needs to understand the study. In most quantitative studies, you will need to provide such information as number, age, ethnic identity, and gender, usually presented in a table. In qualitative studies, the reader expects to find more detailed descriptions of the participants, as in this example:

School District
1. Attendance areas included
2. District organizational structure
3. School board composition and stability
4. Central office staff, including leaders and their tenure
5. Number of students served
6. Grade level organization
7. Number of schools at each level
8. Ethnic composition of student body
9. Number and nature of professional staff
10. Overall student achievement
11. Recent reform activities
12. General nature of parent relationships

School
1. Attendance area
2. Leadership structure and organization
3. Grade levels and student enrollment
4. Student demographics, ethnicity, and nature of special populations
5. Special features of educational programs and curriculum
6. Composition of certified and support staff
7. Testing program
8. Student achievement results
9. Attendance rates
10. Suspension and retention rates
11. Physical condition and appearance of facilities
12. Major concerns and problems
13. Recent reform efforts

Classroom
1. Size, location, physical appearance
2. Student composition: social class, ethnicity, gender, ability
3. Teacher and support staff: attendance, education, experience, gender, ethnicity
4. Student achievement
5. Student attendance and promptness
6. Equipment and materials
7. Curriculum

Community
1. Area covered and general nature of community (urban, suburban, rural)
2. Population: socioeconomic level, ethnicity, political affiliation, population trends
3. Tax base and economic stability
4. Businesses, industries, and social services
5. Major community strengths and problems

Exhibit 16.3. Aspects of the Research Site

Walker Thompson has been teaching English for 30 years. Educated at an Ivy League school and with a master's degree in Renaissance literature, he prides himself on his love of literature. Once married to a woman whom he always describes in generous terms, he is now widowed and lives by himself in a small apartment in downtown Centreville. He is a slight man in physical appearance, but as far as this researcher could determine, never seems to have any trouble in controlling even potentially disruptive students. He speaks with a clear, strong voice even when conversing with colleagues . . .

In quantitative studies, the reader will expect to find details about the selection process, including the following issues: From which population were they selected? What sampling procedure was used, if any? How were they assigned to groups? What previous experience did they have with the content, the instruments, the intervention, or the personnel?

Identify the Instruments Used to Collect Data

A key part of the methodology is the instrumentation used to collect data. The term *instrumentation* is a general one that includes the following:

OBSERVATION INSTRUMENTS: Observation forms; observation guidelines; observation schedules.

INTERVIEWS: Interview protocols (questions to be asked); interview recording devices; interview guidelines.

SURVEYS: Survey form; survey directions.

DOCUMENT ANALYSIS: Document analysis guidelines, criteria.

TESTS AND MEASUREMENTS: Tests used; performance assessment tasks; measurement guidelines.

If you used an existing instrument, you should report on its validity and reliability. If it was an instrument for which you had to secure permission, include in the appendix section the letter granting you permission. If you developed your own instrument, the reader will expect to find an explanation of how you developed it, including how you tested for validity and reliability and what results you obtained. Copies of any homemade instruments should be included in the appendix section.

Explain the Procedures
Used in Carrying Out the Design

Now you explain in a step-by-step manner the procedures you used in carrying out the design. The procedures followed would obviously vary with the type of research. In the standard experimental study, you would probably identify the following steps:

1. Access confirmed
2. Subjects randomly assigned to experimental and control groups
3. Both groups given a pretest
4. Experimental group given the treatment; control group receives no treatment
5. Both groups given posttest

On the other hand, an action research study explaining how a team solved a problem might report the procedures under two main headings.

1. Procedures the team used in solving the problem
2. Procedures the researcher used in studying the team's processes

Regardless of the type of study, you are required to explain the procedures in sufficient detail for two key reasons. First, doing so enables other researchers to replicate the study. Second, doing so enables potential consumers to determine if your findings can be trusted.

Explain How the Data Were Analyzed

All studies will result in a mass of raw data. Thus, a key component of the methodology chapter is explaining to the reader how you handled those data. The data analysis usually includes three procedures.

First, explain how you reduced the data. When you reduce the data, you take the raw data and group it in order to make initial sense of it. In analyzing interview data, for example, a student researcher reported these steps in reducing the data:

1. Transcribing the interviews
2. Reading the transcripts to tentatively identify categories of responses
3. Testing the tentative categories by classifying responses in the first hour of the interviews
4. Using final categories to code all responses
5. Tallying coded responses

Next, explain how you decided to report and display the reduced data. You have several choices of reporting methods: raw data, percentages, mean, median, or standardized scores. You also have several methods for displaying data: narrative text, matrix, tables, graphs, charts, or other figures.

Finally, you explain how you analyzed those data to determine what they meant. In quantitative studies, you report the statistical tests and procedures used; in qualitative studies, you explain how you interpreted the data.

Write a Summary

The final step is to write a brief summary that points out the key features of the methodology and looks ahead to the next chapter. Here is one example: "This chapter has explained the methods used in this qualitative study of one school's attempt to use performance assessments. The next chapter presents the results obtained with those methods."

17

Presenting the Results

In most dissertations, the results are presented in a separate chapter—the fourth chapter. In some qualitative studies, the results are reported in detail in two or three chapters. Regardless of the number of chapters, there are certain strategies you can use.

Prepare for Presenting the Results

Before turning to issues of organization and writing, you should take two preparatory steps. First, review the results carefully. If you used a statistical package, run it again just to check for accuracy. Second, check the style book for the format of tables and figures if you will be presenting some of your data in these forms.

Decide on the Contents and Format of the Chapter

In the initial planning process, review your data and decide the following content and format issues:

- *What will be included in the appendix section of the dissertation?* These materials are typically included in the appendix section: instructions to participants; questionnaires and survey forms; raw data; copies of instruments used; letters of access and permission.

- *What will be included in tables?* In general, tables are used to present complex data in columns and rows. Tables are useful because they present multiple data in a form easy to understand. However, as the APA *Publication Manual* (1994) notes, they also have two disadvantages: Too many tables distract the reader and complicate the processing of text, and too many tables in articles submitted for publication increase the typesetting expense.
- *What figures will be needed?* A figure is any illustration other than a table; the term *figure* includes graphs, photographs, and line drawings. Figures are especially useful in showing nonlinear relationships. A figure should be easy to read and should complement, not duplicate, the text.
- *What are the resulting contents?* All other results will be reported in the narrative text.

In determining the contents of this chapter, you will usually find it to your advantage not to interpret the data. Chapter 5 will include a summary and a discussion; in most dissertations, the "discussion" section is the best place for interpretation. If you include interpretation in the "results" chapter, you will not have much new to say in the final chapter, a more important chapter for the reader.

Determine the Organization of the Chapter

Your decisions about content and format will simplify the development of your outline for the chapter. As with the methodology, you have several choices about the order to use.

- *By hypotheses.* If your study involves research or null hypotheses, you may decide to order by hypothesis: Hypothesis 1, Hypothesis 2, and so on.
- *By research questions.* If your study involved two or more specific research questions, then ordering in terms of those questions would be useful: Question 1, Question 2, and so on.
- *By research method.* If you used multiple methods, grouping the results in relation to the methods may be helpful: Interview results, survey results, and so on.

- *By chronology.* If the time order is important, then organize by chronology: Entry, Middle Phase, Exiting. You can also use a chronological pattern in studies that relied chiefly on testing: pretest results, posttest results.
- *By variable.* If the variables are critical to the study, then order by variable, such as age, self-concept, achievement level.

Obviously, several patterns can work. One way of deciding is to reflect in this manner: "I stated the problem in Chapter 1; I explained my methodology in Chapter 3; I will summarize in Chapter 5. How can I best take my reader from Chapter 3 to Chapter 5?" Also keep in mind the advantages of consistency. If readers find three research questions in Chapter 1, then discover in Chapter 3 that the methodology was presented in relation to those three questions, they will then expect to find the three research questions governing the reporting of results.

Submit your outline to the dissertation chair and make any revisions necessary. Remember that you should always write from an approved outline; doing so will avoid much unnecessary revision.

Develop the Tables and Figures

Before you begin to write the text of the "Results" chapter, make all the tables and figures that you will need. Although it is possible to make the tables and figures as you write the text, you should find it simpler to make the tables and figures first, because doing so will simplify the writing task. The APA *Publication Manual* offers several guidelines for making effective tables, paraphrased as follows:

1. Is the table essential?
2. Is the entire table double-spaced?
3. Is the title brief but clear?
4. Does every column have a column heading?
5. Are all abbreviations and symbols explained?
6. Are notes presented in proper form and order?

Figures also should meet specific criteria: They augment without duplicating the text; they convey only the essential facts, leaving out distracting information; and they are easy to read and understand.

Write the Introductory Paragraph

In writing the introductory paragraph of this chapter, you might find it useful to begin the chapter with a sentence that restates the problem, simply to remind the reader. Then follow that with a sentence that provides an overview of the chapter. Here is an example:

> As stated in Chapter 1, the study reported here examined in detail the problems encountered by teachers as they developed and used performance assessments in their planning and teaching. The chapter is organized in terms of the two specific research questions posed in Chapter 1. It first reports the problems they encountered in developing performance assessments; it then examines the difficulties they experienced in using those assessments in their teaching.

Write the First Section

In general, you will find that this pattern works in writing each section. First, state a generalization that summarizes the results. Then refer to any table or figure that you have developed. Finally, provide the specific evidence. Following is an example, using the contrived table shown in Exhibit 17.1.

Primary Sources Used

> Teachers in 1997 have changed in the primary source used in making long-term plans, as compared with their counterparts in 1986. As indicated in Table 1, more of the 1997 teachers are using the state test as a guide, and fewer are relying upon the textbook and their own knowledge of students. (See Table 1.)

Note that the narrative text does not simply rehash the information presented in the table. Instead, it calls attention to the major findings. The writer assumes that the reader can find in the table all the specific data needed. In writing this and succeeding sections, remember

Table 1. Primary Source Used for Developing Long-Term Plans for
Instruction

Primary Source	1997 %	1986 %
District curriculum guide	12	8
State test	24	12
Textbook	18	26
Teacher's knowledge of students	22	32
Suggestions by colleagues	13	15
Plans from previous year	9	6
Other	3	2

Note: Totals do not equal 100 because of rounding off.

Exhibit 17.1. Example of Table

the importance of objectivity. Report the results without interpreting them or using modifiers that imply a point of view.

Write the Remaining Sections, Using Appropriate Headings

Use that same pattern in writing the remaining sections. Remember to use the various levels of headings to make clear the organization of the chapter. When you have finished writing the main sections of the chapter, write a brief concluding paragraph that notes generally what you have discovered and points the reader to the following chapter. Here is an example:

> The results presented above indicate clearly that the teachers in this study experienced greatest difficulty in using performance assessments as a basis for their teaching. A more detailed summary and a discussion of the findings are presented in the next chapter.

Revise the Chapter and Submit It for Review

In revising the chapter, keep in mind the criteria listed in Exhibit 17.2. They will remind you of the key characteristics desired in this

Does the presentation of results . . .

1. Use an appropriate organizational pattern and make that pattern clear to the reader?

2. Report results accurately and objectively?

3. Effectively integrate text with tables and figures, without unnecessary repetition?

4. Use format for tables and figures as specified by style manual?

5. Emphasize results, without excessive interpretation and discussion?

Exhibit 17.2. Criteria: Presenting the Results

chapter. When you have finished your own revision, submit it to your dissertation chair for his or her review.

18

Summarizing and Discussing the Results

The last chapter of the dissertation is commonly titled *Summary and Discussion*. An older style uses the title *Conclusions and Recommendations*. However, the title presently used seems more accurate, because many studies do not include either conclusions or recommendations.

Review the Results Reported

Begin by reviewing the results of your study. Whereas the previous chapter reported the results in detail, the last chapter reports the general findings. You therefore should review your fourth chapter to identify the general results that should be included in the final chapter. If you have written the "results" chapter in the general-to-specific pattern recommended in this book, you should be able to identify the general results without too much difficulty.

Develop an Outline of the Final Chapter

The outline of the final chapter is different from those for preceding chapters. Because many readers will turn first to the last chapter of your dissertation, you should write it so that it tells the full story of your study. This means that it should include five main parts, as follows:

1. Introduction
2. Statement of the problem
3. Review of the methodology
4. Summary of the results
5. Discussion of the results

In developing an outline for your chair to review, you should provide additional detail for both the summary and the discussion. For example, the outline for the discussion section might look like this:

1. Interpretation of the findings
2. Relationship of the current study to previous research
3. Recommendations for educators
4. Suggestions for additional research

When you have drafted the outline, submit it to your dissertation chair for review.

Write the Introductory Paragraph

The introductory paragraph, like those for previous chapters, should be brief; it should also be presented without any heading. Here is an example of what might be said: "As an aid to the reader, this final chapter of the dissertation restates the research problem and reviews the major methods used in the study. The major sections of this chapter summarize the results and discuss their implications."

Restate the Problem and Review the Methodology

Next, present the problem statement exactly as it appears in Chapter 1. Then review the methodology in sufficient detail, without excessive repetition. Here is an example to illustrate the level of generality:

As explained in Chapter 2, the study reported here was a case study of a principal newly appointed as a replacement for a principal who had been relieved of his duties because of the school's low performance on state tests. As a case study, this research primarily used a qualitative perspective, attempting to discern the meaning of events to the participants. The case study covered the new principal's initial 5 months at the school.

The case study relied chiefly on observations and interviews. The researcher observed the principal for 19 Wednesdays, in each instance spending 6 hours observing the principal in action. Each observation was followed by a debriefing interview; five general interviews were also held, one each month. Four teachers identified by their colleagues as key informants were interviewed on the same day as the general principal interview.

Observe that that review of the methodology provides sufficient information for a reader who has not read the detailed methodology chapter to understand how the study was conducted.

Summarize the Results

In summarizing the results, keep in mind the importance of interchapter consistency. For most dissertations, the statement of the problem in Chapter 1, the explanation of the methodology in Chapter 3, the presentation of the results in Chapter 4, and the summary of the results in Chapter 5 should be organized in a consistent manner. However, any organization of the summary that is approved by your chair and that makes sense to the reader will suffice.

You should find that the general-to-specific pattern works well in summarizing the results: Begin with the general statement and then support it with appropriate details. Here is an example:

> Throughout the entire period of the study, Principal Estevan used a style of leadership that she considered effective but that seemed to confuse the teachers. In all the general interviews, Estevan characterized her style as "flexible" and repeatedly assured the researcher that the school needed a leader who knew how to adjust—to "go with the flow," as she put it. However, the teachers interviewed saw her style differently. In their interviews they frequently used terms such as "inconsistent,"

"uncertain," and "wishy-washy." In contrasting Estevan's leadership style with that of her predecessor, one teacher commented, "With Jenkins, you always knew where you stood; with Estevan, you are never quite sure." Similar sentiments were expressed by three other informants.

Note that the paragraph above begins with a general statement, followed by supporting evidence. However, the supporting evidence is limited to a few relevant specifics; the writer does not wish to present all the details just reported in the previous chapter.

Observe as well that the writer couches the summary in objective language, for the most part avoiding interpretations. Where interpretations are made, the writer uses the word *seems* to indicate tentativeness. Although it is often difficult to separate observations from interpretations, you should do all you can to save the interpretive language for the "discussion" section.

Finally, increase the clarity of the summary section by using appropriate transitional cues. You can use sequencing words, such as *first, also, next, finally*. You can number the general findings in this manner: "1. Students in the experimental group expressed strong dissatisfaction with their insufficient face-to-face contact with the distance instructor." You can also use bullets to highlight your findings, as in this example:

- "Higher levels of student achievement were associated with higher scores on the Index of Community."

Discuss the Meaning of the Study

The "discussion" section of this final chapter is probably the most crucial section of all. Evidence of its importance is the fact that in many scientific reports, the discussion of the findings amounts to one third of the entire report. Many readers will read only this section because they want to know only what the study means. Also, the discussion is your opportunity to bring to bear your own critical intelligence. Although you are still expected to deal with the facts of your study, your readers will expect to hear more of your own voice as you try to make sense of the findings.

Reflect About Your Findings

The process should begin with a time of reflection. One useful way of reflecting is to imagine that you are standing before an audience of your peers. A questioner asks, "Well, aside from all those details, what does your study mean?" Think about the answer you would give if you had only 5 minutes to respond. The ideas that come to you in this time of reflection should help you consider the content of this section.

Determine the Content of the Discussion Section

As indicated above, you should have developed an outline for the entire chapter. If you have not already done so, you should determine the specific content of this section. Although each discussion will vary, certain common elements are frequently found.

Researcher's insights. The reader expects you to make sense of the study, because you were deeply involved in studying it. Your interpretations, however, should avoid sounding too dogmatic. Here is an example of the tone you are trying to achieve:

> On the basis of this study alone, it is difficult to be certain about the factors accounting for Estevan's seeming lack of consistency in style. As noted above, she ascribed it to a desire to be flexible. However, there were subtle signs that her ethnicity may have been a contributing factor. Research by Horton (1998) indicates that a principal who is a member of a minority group will frequently seem tentative in dealing with a faculty that does not include a substantial number of that minority . . .

Relationship of the current study to prior research. You are also expected to relate your findings to previous research. As indicated in the example given above, you may indicate this relationship as you interpret the findings. You may also deal with it in a separate subsection with its own heading. The key issue is to show clearly to the reader how your study builds upon the knowledge base. Here is an example:

> Previous studies of effective principals have concluded that they were especially assertive in their dealings with the faculty during the first semester of their tenure as principal (see, for ex-

ample, Rivers, 1998, and Clemens, 1999). The present study yields a very different portrait of a principal during the "honeymoon" period.

Theoretical implications of the study. It well may be that your study has some major theoretical implications: It may confirm existing theory or present disconfirming evidence. If it does, then you should call attention to these implications, as in this example:

> Bridges's (1967) theory of the "zone of acceptance" would have predicted that these teachers would have been receptive to Estevan's decisions in areas where they had no personal stake. However, the teachers in this study frequently manifested resistance even when the decisions had no immediate impact on them . . .

Explanation of unanticipated findings. If the results of your study seem unanticipated or surprising, the reader will expect an explanation. Here are the sort of factors you might consider: problems with the research design, the use of an exceptional population, sampling errors, mistakes in the control of variables, defects in the instrument, or poor implementation of the treatment. In explaining the unanticipated results, do not apologize for yourself or blame others; simply note the problem. Here is an example of the appropriate tone:

> The fact that the experimental group did not show gains that were statistically significant may have resulted from the teachers' failure to implement the new approach as it had been designed. Discussions with the teachers after the treatment had been implemented indicated that there were major differences in the way they had presented the new unit to the teachers . . .

Implications for practice. Many educational studies will have clear implications for practice. Although you should feel free to make such recommendations, you should again avoid making dogmatic assertions or sweeping recommendations that go far beyond your study. Here is an example of an appropriate way of making effective recommendations:

> Although a single case study cannot provide a sound basis for the practice of leadership, this study (and other case studies with similar findings) would suggest that newly appointed principals should understand that most faculty in such a context

expect changes to be made during the first months of incumbency ...

Recommendations for further research. Finally, you should decide if you should include in this final chapter your recommendations for additional research. In doing so, note only the research that your own study suggests is needed. Some student researchers make the mistake of simply listing an array of interesting topics, many of which have no relationship to their study. Here is how you might accomplish this purpose:

> Additional research seems needed on the ethnic mismatch between principal and faculty. As noted above, it is possible that this mismatch was a factor in Estevan's seeming lack of consistency. Although there have been a few studies of this issue, there is no consistent evidence ...

Write the Discussion Section

In writing the discussion section, do not feel that you have to follow a prescribed order. This section is one place where interchapter consistency is not critical. Tell your story in any way that seems effective, and feel free to be somewhat more subjective.

19

Preparing the Dissertation
for Defense and Publication

You should now be ready to get the dissertation in final shape. This chapter will explain how to prepare it both for your defense and for publication in *Dissertations Abstracts International.*

Secure the Needed Resources

To begin the preparation process you will need to secure three useful resources:

- The style guide you have been using
- Your university's guidelines for the preparation of theses and dissertations
- *How to Prepare Your Manuscript for Publication*, published by UMI Dissertation Services (300 North Zeeb Road, Box 1346, Ann Arbor, MI 48106)

The discussion that follows relies upon the APA *Publication Manual* and the UMI publication. As indicated previously, you should be using whatever style guide your chair recommends. Also note that the UMI publication indicates that the university's guidelines take precedence over UMI's.

Does the dissertation

Format

1. Follow the format specified by the university guide-lines, the style manual, and the UMI publication (in that order of priority)?

Mechanics and Style

2. Use correct spelling and punctuation?
3. Use varied word choice?
4. Demonstrate a mature writing style, avoiding short, simple sentences?

Content

5. Have a clear statement of the problem?
6. Include a review of the research?
7. Explain clearly and completely the methodology?
8. Present the results accurately and clearly?
9. Summarize accurately and objectively the results of the study?
10. Discuss and interpret the results?
11. Make a significant contribution to the knowledge base?

Exhibit 19.1. Editing the Dissertation

Edit the Dissertation

You should use those style guides to do your own editing first. Use the criteria specified in Exhibit 19.1 to make your own corrections. Use the computer to check spelling, make more varied choices of words, and improve style. Then read each chapter very carefully. Look for spelling errors that the spelling checker might have missed. Reread Chapter 12 of this book, using the style reminders to correct any mistakes. Check all your tables and figures for accuracy.

Also keep in mind the preparation guidelines from UMI, as follows:

1. Use high-quality white paper, minimum 20-pound weight, 8 1/2" by 11". Do not use erasable paper.
2. Double-space all text. Long quotations and footnotes may be single-spaced.
3. Use a 10-point or 12-point font.
4. Use a letter-quality printer.
5. Do not use correction fluid or tape.

Most style manuals also recommend that you use a left margin of 1 1/2 inches to provide room for binding.

After you have done your own editing, have someone else use the same criteria to complete a second editing. Even though you might consider yourself a good editor, you need an objective review by someone who is not closely involved with the dissertation. Be sure to note that person's contribution in the "acknowledgments" section (explained below).

Check on Content and Order

As part of the checking process, be sure you include all the elements in the order specified. Most dissertations include the following elements in the order specified below. Each of these is discussed in the sections that follow:

1. Abstract
2. Title page
3. Approval page
4. Acknowledgments page
5. Contents page
6. List of tables and figures
7. Chapters of the dissertation
8. References
9. Appendixes

Some universities specify a different order; be sure to check with the graduate school office or your chair on your university's requirements.

Write the Abstract

The abstract is a summary of your dissertation. You should state the problem and briefly indicate the methodology. You also should summarize the results. In writing the abstract, ask yourself this question: "If I were a researcher trying to decide if this dissertation is worth retrieving, what would I want to know?" In writing the abstract, remember that UMI limits abstracts to 350 words. Do not include tables or figures in the abstract.

Write the Title and Approval Pages

Some universities require separate title and approval pages; some require one page that serves both functions. Check with your chair or graduate office. In choosing a title for your dissertation, keep in mind the needs of other researchers as they do a literature search. Keep the title as brief as possible and be sure it uses terms that will simplify retrieval. Do not use the words *study of* or similar terms. Here are some examples of poor and good titles:

POOR: A Study of Charter School Teachers and Their Motivation to Teach in Charter Schools

BETTER: Charter School Teachers: Reasons for Choosing Charter Schools

POOR: Research Into the Characteristics of Alternatively Certified Teachers as Compared With Teachers Who Were Prepared in Traditional Programs

BETTER: Alternatively Certified Teachers and Traditionally Certified Teachers: Their Distinguishing Characteristics

Write the Acknowledgments Page

The acknowledgments page is the place where you acknowledge all the help you have received. Typically the acknowledgments include thanking the following: the chair, the other committee members, the editor, any funding source, the participants, and family and others. Do not try to be cute or effusive in your thanks. Also, be sure that the chair approves of this section; some chairs report that they are embarrassed by acknowledgments that are too effusive.

Write the Contents Page and Lists of Tables and Figures

Most chairs prefer that in listing the dissertation's contents, you use the heading *Contents*. They do not want you to use the heading *Table of Contents*. It is a table of contents, but the words *table of* are not used in the heading. The same injunction applies to the lists of tables and figures. Use the headings *Tables* and *Figures,* unless your chair wants you to include the terms *List of.*

Include the Chapters

Next, assemble the chapters in order, checking to be sure that the pagination is correct. Also, check with your chair about the style for the chapter heading. Here is the style usually preferred: "1. Introduction to the Study." The word *Chapter* is not included, and there is no underlining. In the terms used in the APA *Publication Manual* , the chapter title is designated as a Level 1 heading.

List the References

The list of references is a crucial part of the dissertation. It requires a special close checking. Here are some guidelines to follow. First, use the heading *References*. Do not use the words *List of* or call it *Bibliography.*

Also, be sure that you have included all the works—and *only* those works—cited in the text. Here is a simple way of checking. Separate the reference pages from the body of the dissertation. Then read each chapter. As you find a reference, check it against the reference list. Are the names spelled correctly and in the proper order? In cases of multiple authorship, are the names listed in the same order? Has the style manual been followed scrupulously? Do all elements of the reference agree? Put a pencil mark next to each one that corresponds.

The pencil marks will enable you to identify references that appear in the text but not in the reference list—and items that appear in the reference list but do not appear in the text.

Include Any Appendixes

Remember that the appendix section includes materials that are better not included in the body of the text. Typically, it includes the following: large tables, a list of terms, samples of instruments, computer programs, and letters of permission or access. A special note about permissions is required here. You should get permission to reproduce any tables or figures. Also, if you use a long quotation, you should check with the copyright holder to determine if permission is needed and if so, request it. Publications vary in their requirements.

Submit the Dissertation

Now you are ready to submit the final dissertation to your chair and the other committee members. When you have also held a successful defense, you will submit it to the graduate school office and to UMI Dissertation Services. UMI will submit your dissertation to the Copyright Office if you wish and will also make it available to other researchers upon request. You should find their manual *Publishing Your Dissertation* a very useful and detailed guide.

IV

Defending and Profiting From the Dissertation

20

Holding a Successful Defense

Your dissertation is ready. Now you face only the defense. How do you prepare yourself for it and conduct yourself during the hearing? These are the questions addressed here.

The answers will, of course, be somewhat influenced by the policies and procedures of your school. The discussion below reflects those in operation at many graduate schools, but you should be sure to determine how hearings are conducted at your school. If possible, attend other dissertation defenses. Also, check with your chair about the following matters: How long will the hearing last? What kind of initial presentation should you make? What role will your chair play? Should you or the chair take detailed notes during the hearing? Will you be able to use technological aids in making your presentation? How will the final results be determined?

Preparing for the Defense

The first suggestion in preparing for the defense is to be sure that you have prepared and distributed to your committee the best possible copy of your dissertation. Procedures will vary here, depending upon your chair's preferences and your school's requirements, but in general, it makes sense to have an excellent draft prepared for the hearing. Even though you probably will have to make changes after the hearing, the good copy will make a more positive impact on the committee. A manuscript replete with errors and strikeovers invites criticism. Arrange matters so that the committee receives the copy 2 to 3 weeks prior to the hearing.

Next, review your dissertation until you know it backward and forward. Know all the major sources you have consulted. Be prepared to explain and defend your methodology. Know what your data mean; be prepared to interpret any tables or figures you have included. Know your last chapter so well that you can almost recite it by heart.

Listed in Resource 20A at the end of this chapter are the kinds of questions you can expect. Think about them in reference to your own dissertation and rehearse the answer you think you might give.

Finally, put yourself in the right frame of mind. You have done your best. If your chair has done his or her work, and if you are able to conduct yourself reasonably well in the hearing, then you know you will pass—and you also know that you probably will be asked to make revisions. But panic and frantic anxiety will not help at this stage. So the night before the hearing, relax, rest, and do whatever else seems appropriate to help you feel at ease in the morning.

Holding the Defense

Arrive at the defense about 30 minutes ahead of time. If it seems appropriate to your chair, arrange to have coffee and pastry available for the committee. Check out the room, find out where you will be sitting, and check all other final arrangements. Greet faculty as they arrive; introduce any who might not know each other. Act as if it is your show and you know how to handle things.

Ordinarily, when all have assembled, the chair will ask you to leave. While you pace the floor outside, the chair is reviewing with the committee the procedures that will be followed. The chair is also using the time to smooth the way for you, because in many ways the chair is also on the spot. You then are summoned to return and the hearing begins.

The defense usually begins with your chair asking you to present your study. Unless your chair advises you otherwise, act as if you are presenting a scholarly paper at a major conference. If possible, avoid using notes. Begin by explaining how and why you became interested in the problem. Discuss briefly the problem as you conceived it. Review your methodology. Focus mainly on the contents of your last chapter by summarizing, interpreting, and discussing your results.

Then the questioning will begin. This, of course, is the most crucial part. You want to respond in a way that suggests you are prepared to enter the community of scholars: You are informed, articulate, suitably humble in the presence of your elders, but quietly confident. Listen closely to each question. If you are unsure about what was asked, either paraphrase or ask for clarification. When you respond, avoid certain common errors that students typically make:

- *Do not become defensive.* If you are asked a question that seems to be a veiled attack, do not respond by counterattacking.
- *Do not apologize or make excuses for yourself.* If someone points out a serious problem, listen, acknowledge the merits of the observation, and indicate that you appreciate the help.
- *Do not blame your chair.* It may well be that your chair gave you some bad advice, but the hearing is not the time to make that known. It is your dissertation; be responsible for it.
- *Do not overstate your case or claim.* Even if you have made a distinguished contribution to the field, let others say that.

After Your Presentation

At an appropriate time, your chair will ask you to leave the room while the committee discusses your defense and ballots on the final decision. When you have left, they will discuss the dissertation and your defense of it. If all is well, they will take only a few minutes to review the changes that must be made and to cast their votes. If there are problems with either the study or your defense, then they will need more time to decide among themselves what action should be taken.

At most universities, committees will make one of three decisions:

1. Dissertation is accepted.
2. Dissertation will be accepted, with minor changes made under the guidance of the chair.
3. Dissertation is not accepted; major changes are required, with final approval by the committee.

When the vote is in and you probably have been told that you have "passed, with minor changes to be made," thank all participants—and, at once, make arrangements to consult with your chair about the changes to be made and the final steps to be taken.

Resource 20A: Questions Typically Asked at Defense

1. Why did you choose that particular problem? Why did you not study this other problem instead?

2. What exactly were you trying to find out? I'm unclear about the meaning of your problem statement.

3. You have reviewed the important literature, but I fail to see what use you make of your review. Can you clarify for me what you learned from the review of the literature?

4. When you reviewed the literature, why did you decide to review that particular area of study?

5. Your review of the literature seems to omit these important contributions. Can you explain why these works and their findings do not appear in your review?

6. Your review of the literature includes this particular work, which is no longer considered a serious contribution. Why did you choose to include that work?

7. I think you may have misrepresented the findings of that study. Could you review for me what you think the study showed?

8. Why did you choose that particular method? Why did you not instead use this other method?

9. Can you clarify for me how the particular method you chose relates directly to the problem you chose to study?

10. What specifically was your relationship to the context and subjects of the study? Do you think that relationship in any way contaminated your study?

11. In what ways was that context or those subjects not representative? Have you been sensitive to that problem of atypicality?

12. Can you clarify for me what procedures you followed to ensure that your research observed the canons of the profession with regard to ethical procedures?

13. I am unclear as to what that table means. Can you interpret it for me?

14. In the text of your dissertation you refer to this particular datum, but I cannot find any table or other support for that figure. Where does it come from?

15. The results you cite on this page seem somewhat in conflict with the results you cite elsewhere. Can you explain the discrepancy?

16. Can you account for this particular result, which seemingly would not have been predicted?

17. You posed certain specific questions in your first chapter. I am not clear that you answered each of those questions. Can you review those specific questions and relate them directly to your findings?

18. Your summary seems just a bit generally stated. Could you speak more specifically about your important findings?

19. I am not persuaded that your conclusions are supported by your findings. Could you explain specifically to me how this conclusion derives from the results of the study?

20. Your recommendations or your discussion of the implications of the study seem too sweeping to me. Can you explain specifically how you arrived at this particular recommendation?

21. If you had 5 minutes to speak to a group of colleagues about the implications of your study, what would you say?

22. If you were doing the study all over again, in what ways would you change it?

23. What are your plans for continuing your research in this area?

24. Can you relate your findings to other important research in the field? In what specific ways do you think you have made a contribution?

25. Your dissertation contains several proofreading errors. Were you aware of those errors?

21

Publishing From the Thesis or Dissertation

As soon as you have successfully defended your dissertation and submitted it to UMI for distribution, you should consider publishing from it. Give serious consideration to publishing in one or more of these three ways: a scholarly paper at a conference, a journal article, or a book.

Present a Scholarly Paper

The first step is to present a paper at a scholarly conference. You should submit a proposal to one of the professional associations in your field. Each association upon request will send detailed guidelines about the forums available, the length of the presentation, and the nature of the proposal desired. Follow those instructions carefully in submitting the proposal based upon your dissertation.

Presenting a paper at a scholarly conference has several advantages. The most important is that doing so will place you in a network of professionals with similar interests. They will learn from you and you from them. It is also a key step in advancing your career, especially if you plan a career in higher education. Finally, it is one major way of contributing to the knowledge base in your field. After presenting a paper at a major conference, you will receive a request from the ERIC staff asking you to submit your paper for inclusion in the ERIC database.

If your conference proposal is accepted, analyze the likely audience. Will most be practitioners or other researchers? The answer will influence how you organize and deliver your paper. Practitioners will expect an emphasis on the practical implications of your study; they will appreciate receiving handouts that they can carry back home.

Here is an outline for a 30-minute presentation to an audience of practitioners.

1. What you learned: 2 minutes (a very general statement as an introduction)
2. Your methodology: 3 minutes
3. A detailed summary of your results: 5 minutes
4. Applications for practice: 20 minutes

Researchers will be more interested in your methodology and the relationship of your research to the existing knowledge base. They will appreciate receiving a copy of the last chapter of your dissertation, formatted as a scholarly paper. Here is an outline for a 30-minute presentation to a scholarly audience.

1. Problem statement: 2 minutes
2. Methodology: 6 minutes
3. Summary of results: 7 minutes
4. Discussion, interpretation, and relationship to prior research: 15 minutes

Regardless of the audience, keep in mind some basic rules of presenting to a large audience.

- *Do not read to them.* You may refer to notes or use a transparency to remind you and the audience of key points.
- *Use effective visuals to supplement the oral presentation.*
- *Err on the side of brevity.* Allow ample time for questions and discussion.

Publish a Journal Article

You should also use your dissertation research as the basis of a journal article. The following steps will help you get your article published.

Identify Several Possible Journals

The first step is to identify four or five journals to which you might submit your article. You should undertake a systematic study of these journals, so that your article fits the journal. This step is a vital beginning step because journals vary in emphasis, audience, length of article, and style.

In analyzing the journal, you may find the form shown in Exhibit 21.1 helpful. The entries in the form will be explained briefly below.

In addition to the journal itself, you should find the following resources helpful:

- *Phi Delta Kappan* periodically publishes an article on writing for publication that contains very useful information on most of the educational journals. Check the most recent article.
- The Richardson and Prickett (1991) manual, *Publication Sources in Educational Leadership*, briefly describes several hundred journals in the field of education.
- *Ulrich's International Periodical Directory* and *Magazines for Librarians* are two references available at university libraries; they both provide useful information about most of the educational journals.
- Several recent issues of the journals you are considering will be useful in helping you analyze the audience, content, and style.

Make a Careful Analysis of Each Journal

Make a systematic analysis of each journal, following these guidelines.

Basic information. Identify the title of the journal, the name of the editor, and the address for submitting manuscripts. Note that

Title:_____

Editor:_____

Address for submitting manuscripts:_____

_____

Frequency of publication:_____

Primary audience:_____

Style guide:_____

Theme issues and dates:

Length of articles:_____

Number of hard copies to be submitted:_____

Disk to be submitted?_____

Refereed?_____

Acceptance rate_____

Decision time:_____

Is a query recommended?_____

Other guidelines:

Exhibit 21.1. Analysis of Journal

smaller journals with part-time editors will have one address for business matters and one address for submitting manuscripts.

Frequency of publication. Note whether it publishes on a monthly, bimonthly, or irregular schedule. Several educational journals do not publish during the summer.

Primary audience. This is a key piece of information. The primary audience is most of the readers who subscribe to the journal. Here are some primary audiences, just as examples: school administrators, classroom teachers, school librarians, or university professors and researchers. The primary audience will affect the organization, content, and style of your article.

Style guide. Each journal has its own style guide, differing chiefly in how references are handled. Some journals use footnotes; some use endnotes; some use citation in text (the method used in this book). You should follow scrupulously the style guide recommended.

Theme issues and dates. Some journals identify a theme for a particular year. For example, the September 1997 issue of *Educational Leadership* is devoted almost entirely to "Teaching for Multiple Intelligences." If you submit an article related to the specified theme, your article will have a better chance of being accepted.

Submission specifications. Note the length of articles published in the journal, the number of hard copies to be submitted, and whether a disk is required (with recommended word processing software).

Use of referees. Scholarly journals send articles submitted to respected authorities in the field, who are called *referees*. These authorities evaluate the article and submit their recommendations to the editor. This information is useful for three reasons. First, refereed journals are much more selective; your chances of being published are therefore limited. Also, if you aspire to a career in higher education, selection committees look closely at the list of publications to determine if the articles were published in refereed or nonrefereed journals. Finally, the editors of refereed journals are slower in their response time, because they must wait for the reports of referees.

Acceptance rate. The acceptance rate is the percentage of articles published, based on the number submitted. Very selective journals might have an acceptance rate of as low as 10%; less-selective journals may publish as many as 80% of the articles submitted. In general, you should submit your first article to a journal with a moderately high acceptance rate, unless you believe that your research is so important that you wish to be published in a journal that is highly selective.

Decision time. Note the time typically required for the editor to make a decision to publish your article. If your article is clearly unfit for that journal, you will usually hear in a few weeks. Most editors will decide in a month or two, but in some cases you may have to wait for as long as 6 to 8 months.

Query recommended. Some journals prefer that you submit a query letter before submitting an article. A query letter briefly describes the article and outlines its contents. Other editors do not wish to receive a query letter; they want to review the article itself as the first step.

Prepare the Article for Submission

Once you have analyzed and identified a few journals that might publish your article, select the one that seems best. Write your article to meet its specifications. In doing so, you should, of course, draw upon your research. However, if you are writing for practitioners, do not follow the organization of the dissertation. Emphasize your summary and discussion, focusing chiefly on its applications for practice.

When you have written your first draft, ask two or three colleagues to critique your article before submitting it. Make the revisions they suggest. Make four copies of the final version—one for you, three for the editor of the journal. Then send the three copies to the editor of the journal, with a very brief cover letter. Indicate that you do not wish to have the copies returned if the article is not selected for publication, unless the journal requires you to send a self-addressed, stamped envelope. Wait patiently. Do not bother the editor with telephone calls or written reminders. Remember that it may take the editor several months to decide.

Do not submit the same article to more than one journal at a time. If your first journal rejects it, revise again and submit to your second choice.

Develop a Plan to Publish a Book

You also should consider using your dissertation research as the basis for a book you might write. You will have to do considerable

1. Author (résumé attached):_____
2. Working title:_____
3. Brief description of book:_____

_____

4. Primary audience:_____
5. Secondary audiences:_____
6. Approximate number of manuscript pages:_____
7. Date for submission of manuscript:_____
8. Analysis of competition:_____

_____

9. Table of contents (attached):_____
10. Sample chapter (enclosed):_____

Exhibit 21.2. Book Plan

work to move from dissertation to book—but the benefits derived are worth the work expended.

The process of developing a plan to publish a book is somewhat similar to that for submitting an article. Begin by identifying and securing copies of the four to six major books in the field in which you hope to publish. Note the publishers of those books, because you probably should *not* submit your plan to them. Most publishers do not wish to publish books that will compete with books on their active list. Next, identify three or four other publishers who publish in that general field but seem not to have published similar works.

Once you have identified some possible publishers, develop a *book plan*. (Some publishers call this proposal a *prospectus*.) The book plan is a proposal you will submit to the publisher to assist the editors in determining if they even wish to consider publishing your book. The typical contents of a book plan are shown in Exhibit 21.2; the major components will be explained briefly below.

Complete the Book Plan

The following components should be included in your book plan:

Author and working title. Note your name and enclose your resume. The *working title* is your tentative title. If your plan is accepted, the publisher will consult with you about the final title, weighing marketing factors.

Brief description of the book. Describe the book in 50 to 100 words. Explain the purpose of the work and its general content.

Audiences. The primary audience is the main readers to whom the book will be marketed. The secondary audiences are others who might read the book. For example, the primary audience for this book consists of graduate students writing a thesis or a dissertation; the secondary audience is the faculty members who advise them.

Book length. Estimate the number of manuscript pages; the publisher can then translate that figure into the number of printed pages.

Submission date. Usually you will be wiser to indicate the number of months after contracts have been signed.

Analysis of competition. This is perhaps the most critical component of the book plan. The publisher wants you to answer this question: "How do we know that the proposed book will sell?" To answer this question, you should develop a form similar to the one shown in Exhibit 21.3. (Exhibit 21.3 shows only part of the form.) The completed form will show at a glance how your proposed work compares with the major competing works. When you have completed that form, you can then comment briefly on the highlights.

Table of contents. Attach a separate page with a detailed table of contents. Do not list only chapter titles; also indicate the major sections of each chapter.

Sample chapter. Usually the editors will want to see a sample chapter as a way of assessing your writing ability.

This Book	Book 1	Book 2	Book 3
Understanding the context for charter schools	x		x
Organizing your constituents	x	x	x
Developing the charter	x	very brief treatment	x
Selecting the staff	x	x	x

Exhibit 21.3. Analysis of Competition

Submit the Book Plan

Ask a colleague to review your book plan. Then select the publisher most likely to publish the book. Do not send it to more than one publisher at a time. Enclose a brief cover letter addressed to the "Acquisitions Editor."

V

Solving Problems Throughout the Dissertation Process

22

Solving Problems
With the Committee

Occasionally, problems develop between the student and the committee—and between members of the committee. To help you deal with such problems, this chapter will clarify the roles of the committee and its dynamics. The chapter then explains how you might both prevent and deal with some of the most common problems.

Roles and Responsibilities of the Committee

You first need to understand the roles and related responsibilities of the committee. As members of your dissertation committee, they are responsible for giving you the direction and assistance you need to complete the dissertation, but that responsibility does not mean that they are supposed to do any of the work for you. It does mean, however, that they should be available to you, within the limits of their other responsibilities. As members of the faculty, they are also responsible to the university to uphold the academic standards of that institution. This means that they cannot accept careless work just to enable you to finish your degree. As researchers-educators, they also feel a responsibility to the larger profession to ensure that the dissertation makes a significant contribution to professional knowledge. As professors, they feel responsible to themselves and their career advancement. They have their own standards of quality—and their own need to advance their careers. Finally, they have several personal roles that cause their own pressures—spouse or partner, parent, and son or daughter.

Obviously, these are conflicting responsibilities that cause conscientious committee members to experience their own stresses. For example, they want to be available to you—but they also need to research and publish if they are to receive tenure and be promoted. Or they want to help you finish in a reasonable time, but they believe that your dissertation needs much more work. They are reluctant to give you criticism that will result in your feeling negative about yourself or them—but at the same time they know your work needs improvement.

If you understand these conflicting responsibilities, you will be better able to deal with committee problems that develop.

Dynamics of the Committee

Each committee will vary somewhat depending upon the personalities of the members. However, three well-documented features of academic life will clearly have an impact on committee dynamics.

First, academic life is hierarchical. As a consequence, dissertation committees are hierarchical, reflecting the status distinctions of academic life. Full professors are at the top. Tenured associate professors come next, followed by nontenured associates. Assistant professors have the lowest status—except for graduate students, who have the lowest status of all. Length of service at the university also affects status: Faculty who have longer periods of service tend to receive higher status than those who have less. These status distinctions suggest that there will be fewer intracommittee conflicts if the chair has higher status than other committee members. If your chair is an associate professor and a committee member is a full professor, the status distinctions might complicate their committee relationships. And the harsh fact is that because you have the lowest status of all, you do not have the power to ignore committee recommendations and decisions.

Also, academic life is individualistic. As a consequence, most committees are fragmented and individualistic. Higher education tends not to reward cooperation and collaboration. Faculty members are promoted and receive tenure chiefly on the basis of their research and publication, with their advising responsibilities having much less weight. These features mean that members have no strong incentives to meet together and work together. Although your committee members may meet with each other at faculty and departmental meetings, they will not be discussing your dissertation at such encounters. In fact, most dissertation committees come together only infrequently, at and prior to defenses. This feature means that you probably have to find ways of working with them as individuals, not as a group.

Finally, academic life is somewhat rigidly structured, with fixed roles and distinctions. This rigid structure usually holds true in committee work. The chair is clearly in charge. The other members understand that their role is to assist, while acknowledging the authority of the chair. It is the chair's reputation that is on the line when your dissertation is reviewed by other faculty, by the graduate school office, and by external members of the profession.

Preventing Problems With the Committee

The key to positive relationships with the committee is preventing problems before they occur. You can do this in several ways. First, choose committee members who are compatible with each other and with you. As explained in Chapter 10, problems of relationships often can be avoided if you are sensitive to the matter when forming a committee.

Second, at a very early stage in your work with the committee, clarify the nature of the committee members' relationships with each other and with you. Most committees are structured in this fashion: The chair does most of the work involved in directing the research and the dissertation and is the primary contact with the student; a second member of the committee provides needed technical expertise; other committee members play a much less active role. Be sure you understand where you are expected to get the help you need—and how much help the committee wants to give you. Learn to use your committee—without taking advantage of them.

Next, determine the specific ground rules by which the committee expects to operate. At the proposal defense or immediately thereafter, you should consult with the chair and the rest of the committee, if necessary, to clarify all important procedural matters. The form shown in Exhibit 22.1 should be helpful here; it has been designed so

1. Name of Student: _____

   Address: _____

   Best telephone contact number: _____

2. Dissertation Problem: _____

3. Type of Study:_____

4. Expected Date of Proposal Hearing: _____

5. Expected Date of Dissertation Defense: _____

6. Name of Dissertation Chair: _____

   Office Hours: _____

   Office Phone: _____ Best time to call: _____

7. Second Member: _____

   Office Hours: _____

   Office Phone: _____ Best time to call: _____

8. Third Member: _____

   Office Hours: _____

   Office Phone: _____ Best time to call: _____

9. Style Guide Preferred: _____

10. Describe briefly how chair prefers to route chapters: _____

_____

11. Ordinarily, how much time will committee need to read and respond to a chapter? _____

12. Describe briefly how chair prefers to handle critique and feedback:_____

_____

13. Identify briefly any professional and academic plans of the committee members that might affect the scheduling of meetings and hearings:_____

_____

14. Other requirements or expectations: _____

_____

Exhibit 22.1. Form for Committee Relationships

that you can complete it after consultation and then give copies to your committee. All the items are self-explanatory, except perhaps those that deal with routing and critiquing. As noted in Chapter 10, you should be sure that you clarify how your chair prefers to have chapters submitted. The routing process will obviously affect the critiquing and feedback process. Here you are essentially determining if the committee members will communicate with you directly or through the chair—and if you will respond directly to their feedback or communicate through your chair.

Selecting a compatible committee and clarifying relationships and procedural matters should obviate most of the difficulties that students encounter with their committees. The other suggestions for maintaining productive relationships with your committee can be summarized briefly.

- *Do not show up for a conference without an appointment.* Most university professors are busy people, contrary to the view of those who think that professors do not have much to do all day. They don't like being surprised by seeing a doctoral student at the office door, chapter in hand.

- *Do not telephone the professor at home, unless directed otherwise.* Most professors prefer to keep academic life and home life separate.

- *Be sensitive to your committee's work schedules and vacation periods.* If you feel you have to give them a chapter to read over the spring break, make suitable apologies.

- *When you mail materials, do so in a businesslike manner.* Put your name and address on all correspondence and manuscripts. Never send original materials through the mail. If it is possible that the professor will have to mail back chapters when he or she is away from the office, enclose a self-addressed, stamped manila clasp envelope. Check with the committee to determine if they prefer to use e-mail for receiving and responding to chapters.

- *Keep your committee informed about progress.* A good general rule is this one: Do not let a month go by without contact. Even a brief note on a postcard or an e-mail message will be useful as a reminder that you are still working.

Dealing With Committee Problems

Even if you have followed all these suggestions, there will still be some predictable problems resulting from the above roles and characteristics that might affect your progress.

Committee Members Do Not Give Feedback Promptly

For most committee members, providing assistance to doctoral students is a labor-intensive responsibility, one that is rather low on their list of priorities. This means that some committee members will be slow in giving you feedback—not because they are irresponsible but because of those conflicting responsibilities. At most graduate schools, the unwritten norm is 2 weeks for committee members to give you feedback. Obviously this will vary, depending upon such factors as the academic calendar, professors' attendance at conferences, and their own involvement in research and publication.

When you experience what you feel are inordinate delays, you should deal with the problem differently, depending upon the source. If other committee members are slow in responding, write them a tactful reminder (without sending a copy to your chair) or telephone your concern. If they still do not respond, then simply report the facts to your chair and let him or her handle the problem.

What do you do if your chair is slow in responding to your chapters? First, as noted above, you should attempt to clarify at the outset how much time is usually required; 2 weeks seems to be an unstated norm. The first few times you experience an inordinate delay, handle the matter as if you're a very tactful bill collector. Call and say, "I'm calling just to be sure you received Chapter 2; I haven't heard and was getting just a bit anxious. When do you think I might be receiving your comments on Chapter 2?" Then if you still haven't heard by the date indicated, call again: "I'm calling just to inquire if there's a special problem with Chapter 2; you indicated that I might be receiving it by today."

If those tactful phone calls do not have their desired effect, then talk over the problem in a face-to-face discussion. Express an attitude that's reflected in these words:

I know you're very busy, and I don't want to make unreasonable demands. However, I am feeling frustrated at my lack of progress. I thought it might be helpful if we could talk the matter over. I want to find out in what way I may be responsible for the delays and take appropriate action.

The rest of the discussion should maintain this problem-solving orientation: "How can we cooperate in order to reduce the turnaround time?"

Committee Members Give Conflicting Advice

Sometimes the conflicting advice is from two different committee members; sometimes it comes from the same professor who changes his or her mind.

If you receive conflicting advice from two members of your committee (including the chair), let the chair handle the matter. Explain the conflict to the chair and ask how you should resolve it. It is the chair's responsibility to mediate such differences; you should not be in the middle.

The problem of receiving conflicting advice from the same individual is a common one. Dissertation students often justifiably complain that after they have revised a chapter according to their chair's (or committee member's) recommendations, they then receive more revision suggestions from the same individual that conflict with those first received. Here is a good process to use that will avoid this frustrating experience:

1. Always check to be sure that you understand the feedback received and have a written record of it. If you meet in a conference, summarize the conference in a written memo and send a copy to the professor: "This is a summary of my notes of the changes we agreed on; I wanted to be sure my record is accurate." If you get a written response, call to clarify any ambiguities. You have to be sure that you understood correctly what the professor wants you to do.

2. When you have revised according to the professor's suggestions, send the professor a copy of his or her suggestions when you submit the revised chapter. That helps the professor remember what was said and reduces the amount of conflicting advice.

Committee Members Give Unhelpful Advice

You may receive what you consider to be unhelpful advice or editorial comments. If the advice or comments are too general, call and ask for specifics. If you feel that you received counterproductive advice about a relatively minor matter, accept it. It is not worth arguing over. However, if you feel that the matter is important, deal with the difference in a professional manner. If the unproductive advice comes from a committee member other than the chair, ask the chair to help you resolve the matter. If the unproductive advice comes from the chair, then meet to review the matter.

Relationships Critically Deteriorate

In a few unfortunate instances, graduate students find that their relationship with the chair or some other committee member deteriorates so badly that they feel the conflict is interfering with their progress. If the conflict is with some member other than the chair, ask for a meeting with just you and the member. In that conference, emphasize that you wish to solve a problem, not complain or blame. Use a problem-solving mode that makes these points:

- I have the impression that there are some serious problems between us. What is your perception?
- I believe these are the specific difficulties. What is your perception?
- These difficulties are causing me some serious problems in my progress.
- How do you think we might solve the problems together?

If that face-to-face conference does not solve the problem, then you should ask the chair to intervene.

If the problem is with the chair, then you should use the same problem-solving approach in trying to resolve the difficulties in a private conference. It is probably unwise to ask another committee member to intercede on your behalf in this instance; doing so may place the member in an untenable position with the chair.

If you are convinced that the chair or a member should be replaced, then be sure to handle the matter professionally. In doing so, keep in mind three useful guidelines:

- *Use a face-to-face discussion, rather than writing.* Writing about a problem usually makes it worse, because it is a one-way communication.

- *Observe the university's chain of command.* Work with a committee member before going to the chair. Work with the chair before going to the department chair. And try to resolve the matter with the department chair before going to the dean of your school. In extreme cases, work with your school's dean before complaining to the dean of the graduate school.

- *Accept the fact that conflict is endemic to the faculty-student relationship.* You each have different perspectives, values, and goals. Differences are bound to arise. Accept all the minor ones as part of your struggle to achieve the degree, and resolve all differences in a professional manner, even when you feel that others are taking advantage of you.

23

Solving Personal Problems
With the Dissertation

You will also experience some personal problems in completing the dissertation. There is a small body of research and a large body of anecdotal evidence indicating that doctoral students experience some common problems throughout the dissertation processes. (For the research, see the following: Council of Graduate Schools, 1991; Germeroth, 1990; Huguley, 1989; Tadeusik, 1989; and Whitted, 1987.) Because the common problems seem to occur at specified times in the dissertation process, they are discussed in this chapter according to the stages during which they usually develop.

These problems can have crippling effects. Some estimates indicate that only 40% of all doctoral students ever finish. Although dropping out is often caused by financial and work-related factors, the emotional stresses involved in completing the dissertation undoubtedly play an important role. For a few students, these stresses will be serious enough to warrant professional counseling; for such individuals, no book can suffice. But for the rest, some rational analysis of the problems and their solutions might be useful.

There seem to be four crucial periods when doctoral students tend to experience serious emotional problems that relate to the dissertation: near the end of the coursework; after completing coursework and before writing the proposal; after the proposal hearing; and after the dissertation defense.

Problems Near the End of Coursework

A large proportion of doctoral students drop out near the end of their coursework. In many instances, the reasons are valid, and dropping out is the wiser choice. They change career plans, choosing to follow a career where the doctorate is not essential. Their values and their priorities change; they decide that family, job, or personal enjoyment is more important than the prestige of having the doctorate. And many simply run out of money: Graduate education is becoming so expensive that many of the most promising students are withdrawing because they have grown tired of mortgaging their futures. But others withdraw primarily for emotional reasons, and it is fear most of all that gives rise to the problems at this stage. From lack of knowledge and from their own insecurity, many doctoral students have come to fear the dissertation. They may try to conceal this fear by pretending that the degree is unimportant and the dissertation absurd, but it is there all the time, regardless of the forms it takes. There are several specific fears.

"I'm afraid that the dissertation will just take too much time." This is a general fear that seems to color all other feelings. The dissertation seems like an impassable mountain. You probably have heard stories of students who have struggled for years without ever finishing. To a certain extent, this fear also is justified; from choosing a topic to defending the dissertation can take as long as 2 or 3 years for part-time students. However, even a complex project like writing a dissertation can be accomplished efficiently with careful planning and conscientious effort. It is like a long journey that you make one step at a time.

The scheduling suggestions offered in Chapter 5 should help you cope with this particular anxiety. In addition, the following suggestions should help:

- Follow the schedule, even if it means making other adjustments.
- If you encounter obstacles, get the help you need.
- Break larger tasks into smaller steps.
- Keep in close touch with your academic adviser and dissertation chair.

"I'm afraid I don't have what it takes to do the dissertation." This is also a reasonable fear, because writing the dissertation is a demanding task.

The way to deal with the fear is to assess your capabilities as objectively as you can, with the help of a faculty member whom you respect and who knows you. Do not ask a spouse or a friend, "Do I have what it takes?" You probably will receive only well-intentioned encouragement.

Instead, do a systematic assessment of your strengths and weaknesses with input from someone who can be honest with you; the form in Exhibit 23.1 might be of help to you here. If you identify deficiencies, take steps to remedy them, if they seem remediable.

"I'm afraid of what the dissertation will do to my family and social life." There is also a modicum of rationality in this anxiety. Dissertations take time, money, and psychic energy—and many relationships have been strained during dissertation time. Here again, there is an obvious solution. Instead of simply worrying about the matter, discuss it openly with your spouse or partner. Examine together what mutual advantages will accrue with receiving the degree and what sacrifices must be made. How much will the dissertation cost in terms of money—and where will the money come from? How will doing the dissertation affect the contributions you can make to child-drearing and household maintenance? Can your spouse or partner understand and accept the fact that you will often seem distracted, absorbed, moody, and perhaps irritable, especially on those bad days when you get back a chapter your chair has rejected?

"I'm worried about the financial costs of doing the dissertation." The budgeting process suggested in Chapter 1 should be of help here. Be realistic about the costs of doing the dissertation and about the resources available to you.

"I'm worried about the impact on my professional assignment." At the outset of the entire process, discuss your plans with your supervisor, without asking for special treatment. If it seems feasible, choose a research topic that will be of help to your organization. As you experience conflicts between writing the dissertation and doing your job, try to find win-win solutions by making compromises and adjustments.

There are some real fears to be confronted and dealt with, but they are all surmountable.

Doctoral student's name: _____

Assessor:_____

Directions: The student named above would like your candid assessment of his or her specific abilities as they relate to completing the dissertation. For each crucial skill or trait listed below, circle one of the following:

   NP: No problem here with this skill

   IN: Some improvement is needed here—but the skill or trait can be remedied

   SD: Seriously deficient; the deficiency seems so serious that it may be a major stumbling block

Skill or Trait	Your Rating
1. **Work habits**: can set and stick to a work schedule; can work for long periods of time without close monitoring or direction; can work efficiently without wasting time.	NP IN SD
2. **Writing**: can write good academic prose; knows conventions of academic writing; can write clearly.	NP IN SD
3. **Organizing and planning**: can set long-term and short-term goals; can develop systematic plans to meet those goals; can take corrective action when problems are encountered.	NP IN SD
4. **Research**: understands the limitations and uses of the research method selected; can use that research methodology in scholarly fashion without close monitoring.	NP IN SD
5. **Intellectual**: reasons logically; understands complexities of research issues; can critique and synthesize the research of others; can learn from experience.	NP IN SD
6. **Interpersonal**: takes criticism well; accepts direction when necessary; is sensitive to faculty priorities.	NP IN SD

Exhibit 23.1. Crucial Dissertation Skills and Traits

Problems at the End of Coursework

Another critical period is after you have completed the coursework and before you get to the proposal stage. Students who drop out here are the army of the "ABDs"—All But Dissertation. Again, there are often practical reasons operating: lack of money, change of plans, the onset of health problems. More often, however, the problems are emotional and psychological ones—and the problems at this stage all seem related to a pervasive anxiety that results in prolonged procrastination. Notice how this student put it, in a candid letter to a friend who asked about his progress:

> I've been paying my dissertation fees for five terms now and I still don't have a proposal ready. I keep promising myself that this will be the term when I get the proposal in shape—but I never make it. I just can't seem to get a fix on a good problem—everything important either has been studied already—or is too big for me to handle. I make lists of problems—but nothing clicks. I talk to the professors and each one suggests a different problem until I'm completely confused. And I don't think I have the research skills I need; I have always been weak in statistics. I guess to be honest that if I did find a problem and could feel positive about my skills, I would still have trouble developing a proposal—I just don't know where to begin. Some students talk about 150-page proposals. How could I ever write 150 pages about what I will study?

Such a statement reflects anxieties that most ABDs have at one time or another. Aside from being colored by the same general fears described above, the statement reveals some specific concerns about the topic, the research skills, and the proposal. And how to deal with these specific concerns is to a great extent the focus of this entire work. However, some general guidance can be offered at this point for dealing with dissertation anxiety and the resultant sense of being immobilized.

1. *Decide once and for all if you want the doctoral degree.* If you don't, withdraw gracefully, consoling yourself with the fact that most great leaders and artists never had a doctorate. If you do want the degree, then make the necessary plans—and carry them out.

2. *Find one professor who is willing to work with you as a chair.* At a certain point, some students can be helped by talking with several professors, sounding them out about research problems and methodologies. But if you are stuck at the preproposal stage, you are probably better off going to one professor whom you hope will be your chair. Be candid about your problem: "I'm having trouble getting to the proposal stage. I'd like to work with you, but I'll need your help in getting myself organized." Then listen to that one professor; talking to several about possible topics and methods will only confuse and delay you.

3. *With the assistance of your chair and this book, choose a topic that you want to study and settle on the methodology.* Stop thinking about the 10 topics that you might study; settle on one. And don't become obsessed with finding the perfect topic. Like the perfect spouse, it doesn't exist.

4. *Read a few completed dissertations on a topic of interest.* It helps to see some completed works to gain a realistic perspective about the dissertation. You may also get some ideas that will stimulate your thinking.

5. *Develop any skills that need sharpening.* If you feel a bit weak with the research method, get the necessary tutoring or instruction. If you are unsure about your writing skills, find out what services the university provides to students needing assistance.

6. *Develop a schedule and stick to it.* By conferring with your chair and applying what you learn in this book, work out a realistic schedule and force yourself to meet the deadlines you have set.

Your choices are clear: You can withdraw gracefully; you can continue to enrich the university's coffers by paying your fees without making progress; or you can get your act together. It is as simple as that. Just stop making excuses for yourself.

Problems After the Proposal

All students writing dissertations experience several emotional highs and lows. Your data gathering goes well, and you feel euphoric.

You get a chapter back with some caustic criticisms, and you feel crushed. A good part of being able to deal with the emotional problems encountered during the dissertation itself is knowing what form they will take and being prepared to deal with them. For the most part, the problems at the dissertation stage seem to be ones of doubt and uncertainty that take the form of predictable complaints.

"I'm tired." Physical and psychic fatigue are common complaints; you just get very tired collecting data, sitting at the desk, pounding the keys. Your head starts to hurt, and you find yourself feeling irritable. You know the answers to fatigue: Eat sensibly, exercise, get adequate rest, and reward yourself with a day off now and then.

"The data gathering is not going well." All researchers, from the beginner to the expert, encounter predictable problems with the research itself. Questionnaires are not returned; subjects drop out of the study; instruments do not work as they should; the data don't act the way you predicted. The answer to such problems, obviously, is immediate communication with your chair. Do not wait, hoping things will clear up; even if they do, your chair will want to know about and assist with the difficulties as they develop. Also, do not avoid confrontation, fearing that your chair will tell you to scrap the whole thing. Good chairs know how to salvage studies that start to go wrong. In a scientific sense, there are no failures in well-designed studies; "no significant difference" may be truly a significant finding.

"I keep finding references in the literature I want to cite." It is a wise idea to keep abreast of current research as you do your study, but once you have reviewed the research for your dissertation, there usually is no need to add very current references. You can add current references to your own files and review them prior to the hearing, but it would be unwise to go on revising the literature chapter once it has been approved—unless you come across some truly important study that just cannot be ignored. Confer with your chair to set a reasonable date for concluding the search of the literature.

"I will be the last of my cohort to finish." Such comparisons are inevitable but irrelevant. Writing a dissertation is not like running a

race. All that matters is the quality of the work. Four or 5 years from now, no one will remember who finished first and who finished last.

"I now feel that I chose the wrong topic." This doubt seems to beset all doctoral students at some point. Just remember that there is no right topic and get on with concluding your study of the one you chose.

"I have writer's block and can't write." Dry periods come to all who write. The best answer for writer's block is to write. Sit at the word processor and force yourself to write, even though the product is not of the highest quality. You can always go back and revise. What you should not do about writer's block is worry about it while you find excuses for not writing.

"I'm worried sick about the defense." Reassure yourself with the knowledge that very few students fail the defense; a good chair won't let you go to the defense until he or she is sure you are ready. Also, if you follow the suggestions in this book, you should have no problems at the defense. It will seem more like a final ritual of celebration than a test.

Note that most of those complaints seem to have a common thread of self-doubt. And that self-doubt is understandable. You feel tired. The end is not yet in sight. You are not getting much positive feedback. You seem close to the end of your resources. You are like a runner who feels tired at the halfway mark. At such a time you need to turn to whatever support is available—your peers, your chair, your spouse or partner, your spiritual director—to help you find the inner resources to continue. Most doctoral students find support in networking with others at the same stage.

Problems After the Defense

Most students find it difficult to believe that there can be any emotional problems after the defense, but many who have gone through the experience talk about the period right after the defense as a time of "postpartum depression." It seems to be a general sense of emptiness, of bleak uncertainty.

The causes are understandable. There is first a predictable let-down. The doctoral degree really has not changed things, and having "doctor" in front of your name has not markedly increased the respect that people accord you. You probably face some career dislocation. You pursued the doctorate because you wanted to advance professionally. Now you have the degree, and you face the trauma of job-hunting. And there is often a sense of emptiness in each week. A major intellectual task that gave your days an organizing center is finished, and you have all that time now to use in some productive fashion. Maybe you are now no longer the center of attention in the household; that patient spouse or partner who sacrificed for so long now expects you to carry more than half the load. And you take a look at your dissertation in its new binder and shake your head in dismay: It really wasn't worth it after all.

The best way out of such depression is usually through meaningful action. After a suitable period of self-indulgence, decide what you want to do next professionally. Will you follow up on your research? Will you publish from your dissertation? Will you try to develop a part-time consulting role? Will you actively seek a new position? Then make the plans that will help you accomplish what now seems important to you.

References

American Psychological Association. (1990). Ethical principles of psychologists (amended June 2, 1989). *American Psychologist, 45,* 390-395.

American Psychological Association. (1994). *Publication manual of the American Psychological Association* (4th ed.). Washington, DC: Author.

Apple, M. W. (Ed.). (1997). *Review of research in education 22.* Washington, DC: American Educational Research Association.

Broadfoot, P., & Osborn, M. (1987). Teachers' conceptions of their professional responsibility: Some international comparisons. *Comparative Education, 23*(3), 287-301.

Burden, P. (1990). Teacher development. In W. R. Houston (Ed.), *Handbook of research on teacher education,* 311-328. New York: Macmillan.

Cochran, W. (1977). *Sampling techniques* (3rd ed.). New York: John Wiley.

Council of Graduate Schools. (1991). *The role and nature of the doctoral dissertation.* Washington, DC: Author.

D'Andrea, L. M. (1997). *Obstacles to completing a doctoral program.* Unpublished manuscript, University of Nevada, Reno.

Dilworth, M. E. (1991). *Motivation, rewards, and incentives.* Washington, DC: American Association of Colleges for Teacher Education.

Flood, J., Jensen, J. M., Lapp, D., & Squire, J. R. (Eds.). (1991). *Handbook of research on teaching the English language arts.* New York: Macmillan.

Germeroth, D. (1990, November). *Lonely days and lonely nights: Completing the doctoral dissertation.* Paper presented at the annual meeting of the Speech Communication Association, Chicago.

Glatthorn, A. A. (1990). *Supervisory leadership.* Glenview, IL: Scott Foresman.

Glickman, C. D. (1981). *Developmental supervision.* Alexandria, VA: Association for Supervision and Curriculum Development.

Goetz, J. P., & LeCompte, M. D. (1984). *Ethnography and qualitative design in educational research.* New York: Academic.

Hoy, W. K., & Miskel, C. G. (1987). *Educational administration: Theory, research, and practice.* New York: Random House.

Hubbard, R. S., & Power, B. M. (1993). *The art of classroom inquiry.* Portsmouth, NH: Heinemann.

Huberman, M. (1989). The professional life cycle of teachers. *Teachers College Record, 91*(1), 31-57.

Huguley, S. (1989). An investigation of obstacles to completion of the dissertation and of doctoral student attitudes toward the dissertation experience (Doctoral dissertation, Pepperdine University, 1988.) *Dissertation Abstracts International, 50,* 372-A.

Janis, I. L., & Mann, L. (1977). *Decision making: A psychological analysis of conflict, choice, and commitment.* New York: Free Press.

McLaughlin, M. W., & Talbert, J. E. (1990). The contexts in question: The secondary school workplace. In M. W. McLaughlin, J. E. Talbert, & N. Bascia (Eds.), *The contexts of teaching in secondary schools* (pp. 1-16). New York: Teachers College Press.

McMillan, J. H. (1996). *Educational research: Fundamentals for the consumer* (2nd ed.). New York: HarperCollins.

Meloy, J. M. (1994). *Writing the qualitative dissertation.* Hillsdale, NJ: Erlbaum.

Merriam, S. B. (1988). *Case study research in education: A qualitative approach.* San Francisco: Jossey Bass.

Miles, M. B., & Huberman, A. M. (1984). *Qualitative data analysis.* Beverly Hills, CA: Sage.

Morgan, D. L. (1997). *Practical strategies for combining qualitative and quantitative methods.* Portland, OR: Portland State University.

Phelps, L. A., & Hanley-Maxwell, C. (1997). School-to-work transitions for youth with disabilities. *Review of Educational Research, 67,* 197-226.

Richardson, M. D., & Prickett, R. L. (1991). *Publication sources in educational leadership.* Lancaster, PA: Technomic.

Rudestam, K. E., & Newton, R. R. (1992). *Surviving your dissertation.* Newbury Park, CA: Sage.

Seczko, M. M. (Ed.). (1996). *The foundation directory* (18th ed.). New York: Foundation Center.

Smith, M. L., & Glass, G. V. (1987). *Research and evaluation in education and the social sciences.* Boston: Allyn & Bacon.

Sprinthall, N. A., & Thies-Sprinthall, L. (1983) The teacher as adult learner: A cognitive-developmental view. In *Staff development* (Eighty-Second Yearbook of the National Society for the Study of Education). Chicago: University of Chicago Press.

Tadeusik, C. J. (1989). Stress and coping among first-year doctoral students (Doctoral dissertation, University of North Carolina, Chapel Hill, 1988). *Dissertation Abstracts International, 49,* 3670-A.

Wehmeyer, L. B. (1995). *The educator's information highway.* Lancaster, PA: Technomic.

Whitted, J. (1987). Ph.D. candidates' stresses and strains related to their dissertation process (Doctoral dissertation, University of Michigan, 1987). *Dissertation Abstracts International, 48,* 1402-A.

Yin, R. K. (1989). *Case study research: Design and methods.* Newbury Park, CA: Sage.

Index

CORWIN
PRESS

The Corwin Press logo—a raven striding across an open book —represents the happy union of courage and learning. We are a professional-level publisher of books and journals for K–12 educators, and we are committed to creating and providing resources that embody these qualities. Corwin's motto is "Success for All Learners."